They Say
My Kid's Gifted:
Now What?

Ideas for Parents
for Understanding and Working
With Schools

They Say My Kid's Gifted: Now What?

Ideas for Parents for Understanding and Working With Schools

A Service Publication of the
National Association for Gifted Children

F. Richard Olenchak, Ph.D.

The National Association for Gifted Children
1707 L Street, NW, Suite 550
Washington, DC 20036
(202) 785-4268
http://www.nagc.org

A Service Publication of the
National Association for Gifted Children

Prufrock Press, Inc.
P.O. Box 8813
Waco, Texas 76714-8813
(800) 998-2208
FAX (800) 240-0333
http://www.prufrock.com / Prufrock@prufrock.com

Table of Contents

Forward

The educational needs of students who are gifted and talented are very real—particularly if you are the adult charged with rearing one. Although schools in approximately half of the states are required by state legislation to identify and provide programs appropriate to the needs of able youth, the variations on the theme are enormous. While certain school provisions should, in fact, be made based on the educational requirements of each *individual* student, there are some characteristics and components of programs that should be in place for virtually all students who wear the gifted and talented label.

The purpose of this book is to provide parents an easy-to-use guide for negotiating the educational bureaucracy *after* having had a child identified for gifted and talented educational services. Due to the fact that identification of bright students for such school programs typically occurs during the elementary and middle school years, the text is oriented toward parents of children between approximately 5 and 14 years of age. However, there are a number of pointers that have application beyond middle school and into the senior high school grades.

Having served for years in a variety of public and private education positions, including that of principal of both elementary and middle schools, the information contained in this handbook is based in reality and practicality. It is actually a map for maneuvering through school systems that has been designed from the inside looking out; it might be called the "Rand McNally" for parents of gifted and talented youngsters. As a result, the focus is always on moving from the place where you are presently with regard to education of gifted and talented students to a place that I hope is more appropriate for your own gifted and talented child.

I. The Double-Edged Sword:

Identification of the Gifted and Talented and What It Means for Parents

Identification of gifted and talented children is truly a controversial issue. Despite years of research, there are some significant disagreements among professional educators and psychologists about the label itself, what it means, and how to identify giftedness. Thus, the ways in which children are ultimately identified vary greatly from state to state, from community to community, and even from school to school.

Generally, most professionals accept the notion that gifted and talented children possess an array of characteristics that assist teachers and parents in identification. When children are very young, even before admission to formal preschool programs, it is not unusual for parents to be the first to begin recognizing differences among children. Occasionally, such differences are noticeable among children in a single family, but it is more likely that parents of very young children will begin to recognize differences between their child and other children who are approximately the same age.

As a result, many lists of characteristics of gifted and talented children have been developed to assist parents and teachers in identification. The unfortunate part of these well-intentioned lists is that many parents and professionals abuse them; somehow, users fail to heed the disclaimers cautioning that the

1

lists are not comprehensive. In addition, there is a tendency to exclude youngsters from further consideration because they do not manifest *all* of the traits listed. In fact, very few children will satisfy all of the characteristics on any list. The lists should serve as guidelines, not definite "must have's" that are etched in stone. Table 1 on page 82 presents a list of characteristics that is divided by the different types of gifts and talents included in the original federal definition discussed below.

Parents must keep in mind that, while the lists of characteristics can be helpful in framing at least a tentative picture of the kinds of behaviors and activities gifted children are likely to demonstrate, lists tend to offer only an overview. There are many different kinds of gifts and talents, some of which schools choose to serve and some of which remain unserved (Gallagher, 1985; Gallagher & Gallagher, 1994).

Definitions vs. Realities

Gifted and talented students currently are not addressed by federal mandates that require educational services for children in nearly all other categories of exceptionality. For the most part, federal educational mandation for other exceptionalities guarantees that programs are offered and programming across state and local jurisdictions vary only within a certain narrow range of professionally accepted parameters. In contrast, federal and some state legislation aimed at the educational needs among gifted and talented students is more permissive in nature; for example, Connecticut passed legislation pertaining to gifted and talented students many years ago, but the state law requires only that schools identify such students and does not contain any language compelling schools to provide specialized programs. Federal legislation to date (described later in this chapter) is also permissive in nature and not mandatory. Hence, the range of services provided and the definitions

2

that steer identification as well as programs vary significantly across the United States. It is feasible for a youngster to be identified as gifted and talented in one location and not qualify elsewhere. The definitions used can be, at least in part, responsible for such incongruities. Fortunately, sensibility prevails in most communities, and students who have been identified in one place generally are included in gifted and talented programs in other locations. If a family is about to relocate, this issue should be investigated before selecting a new school.

In some states, identification and services for gifted and talented children are strictly determined within each local school district and, in some cases, within the local school itself. It is important for parents to learn whether it is the school district or the local school that identifies and serves gifted and talented students, and also to discern the precise nature of those definitions and services. Some school districts in a state may identify and serve gifted students, while others do not. On an even smaller scale, single schools within the same school system may elect to identify and serve gifted students, while others decide not to do so. Moreover, some schools may define giftedness in terms of high intellectual/academic ability, while others may define giftedness as artistic talent and thereby choose to identify and serve only those students with a high degree of artistic ability. These differing definitions dictate differing types of identification. Again, parents should determine these factors before relocating.

Because some states have mandated services for gifted and talented children, identification and services are likely to be related to specific definitions that apply throughout an entire state. This creates some degree of consistency in identification and in programs, though not entirely. Even with mandates, some states allow schools or whole school districts to identify and serve only certain kinds of gifts. The situation is further confused by the fact that parents often assume that state laws require the same types of identification and service from state to state. Nothing could be further from the truth. In fact, even in states that are located in the same geographic area and where provisions for gifted and talented education are required, there is no guarantee that identification methods and programs will be the same. It is wise to check with state departments of education and local school systems about the types and availability of programs for gifted and talented students.

Parents must determine what definition of giftedness is used by the state (in states where there is a mandate), or by the school system or school (where there is no state mandate), and then whether or not the identification and programs the school provides match the definition. Although it seems logical that definitions, identification, and services should agree, do not assume that a school system that has elected to define giftedness on a broad scale (i.e., defines giftedness in terms of many types of abilities) necessarily will identify and then provide school-related programs for each of those kinds of abilities (Pendarvis, Howley, & Howley, 1990, p. 323).

For example, consider a school system located in a midwestern state that has no required definition, identification, or services for gifted and talented children. Given the great deal of freedom extended to local schools in such a case, this school district elected to define gifts and talents broadly in accordance with the 1972 report to the U.S. Congress (see "Federal Definition" on page 5). Seemingly, procedures should have been used to identify and then serve children in each of the types of giftedness mentioned in that definition. In practice, however, the school district identified children in only a few of the gifts and talents mentioned in the definition, and actually served only two of those. With no state or federal law upon which to rely, parents had no recourse; even if a child had been identified, there was no guarantee the child would be served within the scope of the school curriculum.

Federal Definition

Despite the fact there is no federal requirement for the identification and specialized instruction of gifted and talented students, there has been work at the federal level to define gifts and talents. The 1972 Marland Report to Congress defined gifted and talented children as:

> those identified by professionally qualified persons who, by virtue of outstanding abilities, are capable of high performance. These are children who require differentiated educational programs and services beyond those normally provided by the regular school program in order to realize their contribution to self and society. Children capable of high performance include those with demonstrated achievement and/or potential in any of the following areas:
>
> ◆ General intellectual ability
> ◆ Specific academic aptitude
> ◆ Creative or productive thinking
> ◆ Leadership ability
> ◆ Visual and performing arts
> ◆ Psychomotor ability. (Marland, 1972, p. 2).

This definition is important because it has served as a cornerstone for the vast majority of state definitions. Well over half of the states, whether they have mandated gifted education or not, include in their state definitions most of the abilities mentioned in the original Marland explanation (Council of State Directors of Programs for the Gifted, 1985; 1991). However, in 1978, the federal definition eliminated "psychomotor ability" from among the areas of gifts and talents because there was already a great deal of effort

5

targeted at psychomotoric talents through various school athletic programs.

Since that time and with the closing of the U.S. Office for the Gifted in 1981, there was no significant activity at the federal level regarding gifted education until the passage in 1989 of the 1988 Jacob K. Javits Gifted and Talented Students Education Act (P.L. 100-297). The U.S. Office for the Gifted was then reopened, though its role has not been broadened in any significant way due to the fact that there is still no federal requirement to provide appropriate educational opportunities for gifted and talented students. One of the primary functions of the office is to provide financial assistance to state and local educational agencies, institutions of higher education, and other public and private agencies and organizations that provide educational services to gifted and talented students. This is accomplished through a series of special projects meant to serve as models for others to replicate. Moreover, the federal definition is evolving, indicative of the permissive nature of the Javits legislation as distinct from the mandatory type described earlier in this chapter. One of the most recent definitions of gifted and talented students appeared in the *Federal Register* of March 13, 1992:

> *Gifted and Talented Students* means children who:
> 1. give evidence of high performance capability in such areas as intellectual, creative, artistic, or leadership capacity or in specific academic fields; and
> 2. require services or activities not ordinarily provided by the school in order to develop those capabilities fully. (*Federal Register*, 1992, p. 8997).

Definitions, Identification, and Recent Research

As the federal definition indicates, there has been a gradual movement toward defining gifts and talents in a more comprehensive fashion and away from the view of giftedness as simply a high degree of general intelligence, as was the case prior to the Marland Report. During the late 1970s and early 1980s, increased efforts to examine giftedness resulted in several behavioral views, including those of Joseph Renzulli, who has been especially influential. He broadly defined gifts and talents in terms of an interaction among three clusters of human abilities: above average ability, creativity, and task commitment (1977, 1978, 1985). When these clusters of human traits interact and are brought to bear upon some area of performance, gifted behavior is the result (Renzulli & Reis, 1985, p. 28). Identification of giftedness employing this definition focuses to some extent on stimulating gifted behavior in children (identification through behavior) by involving them in an array of highly-organized activities likely to trigger the behavioral interaction. Note that in this conception of giftedness the definition, identification, and programming are clearly linked.

Similarly, several psychological researchers have been involved in examinations of human intelligence. These studies have pointed to the fact that humans possess multiple intelligences and, as such, are capable of differing types of giftedness. The works of Gardner (1983, 1985, 1993) and Sternberg (1982, 1985, 1986, 1988) have uncovered a number of ways in which people can excel. Moreover, these models promote identification of and programming for a wide range of gifts and talents, few of which are identifiable through traditional tests. As in the Renzulli approach, definition, identification, and programming are in agreement.

Meanwhile, a great deal of research has been conducted about the Talent Search programs, a nationwide program that uses early results (seventh grade in most cases) of the Scholastic Aptitude Test (SAT) or the American College Test (ACT) to identify mathematically and verbally precocious youth (Benbow & Stanley, 1982, 1983; Stanley, 1985). These studies

7

have shown reliably that, for youth judged as gifted because of their SAT or ACT performance, accelerated educational programs are appropriate in the areas in which precocious ability was demonstrated on the test. Once more, definition, identification, and programming complement one another.

For parents, the recent research has one major implication: the definition used by a school or school district, the identification methods, and ultimately the program provided for gifted and talented students must agree. Otherwise, definitions, identification, and program curriculum may be meaningless to the very children for whom the efforts were originally intended. It is crucial that discerning parents investigate the relationship among definition, identification, and curriculum in gifted and talented programs. A high degree of relationship probably indicates that the school maintains a well-planned, purposeful gifted and talented program.

How Did We Get Here?

Regardless of the effects recent research efforts have had on definitions and the identification process, nearly all schools use a four-step process for identification based on that utilized with students who have other kinds of exceptionalities. This process consists of: 1) referral; 2) assessment; 3) determining eligibility; and 4) placement.

Generally, referrals may come from any person who knows the child and has reason to believe the youngster would benefit from or needs involvement in the gifted and talented program. Referrals in many schools are accepted from parents as well as teachers and other professionals. In addition, some schools accept peer- and self-nominations. Most schools use a checklist or other type of referral form.

Assessment varies greatly, depending on the definition and the types of gifts and talents a school seeks to identify. While individual IQ tests certainly have their value, they will provide little useful information for the identification of students who excel outside of the intellectual or academic realm. Furthermore, IQ tests are limited in that they do not truly measure all of the complexities of intelligence; rather, they are helpful in assessing academic aptitude in a given culture, usually that of the majority (Borland, 1986). Other kinds of tests typically used in assessing gifted and talented children include group intelligence tests, achievement tests, and tests of creativity. A number of schools also employ observations and interviews of children as means for assessing educational needs.

Usually, a committee in each school or school district determines eligibility of students for gifted and talented programs. There is a specific attempt to decide whether or not the student can benefit from or needs the gifted and talented program in order to enhance his or her schooling. If it is determined, based on the assessment, that the child qualifies, in most cases the committee will notify and possibly meet with the parents to explain the child's placement in the program. In a few states, programs are required to be tailored to each student, as federal legislation demands for other exceptionalities. In those circumstances, the specific activities in the program may be detailed in the form of an Individualized Education Program (IEP), much like those used with students in programs for other exceptionalities. The IEP, usually designed on an annual basis, defines specific goals and objectives for a child's program participation.

Wearing the Label: Now What?

Once a child has been identified and that information is shared with the family, the child's social community, and the social community of the parents, parents will have some work to do. What does it mean to be gifted? Will our whole family change? What can a parent do for such a child?

9

While there are no easy answers, there are several things parents can do to maintain an even keel. The following strategies should be used to assist both the child and the parents in handling the gifted label:

1. **Educate yourself:** Parents should learn as much as possible about gifted and talented children and the educational opportunities that are appropriate to the *individual* needs of their own child. To group *all* gifted and talented children together as if they were exactly the same is as wrong as grouping every flower in a large garden together simply because they are all flowers. Just as each variety of flower requires sunlight, fertilizer, and water to grow, each gifted and talented child needs love, understanding, and instruction in order to flourish. Each flower must have varying amounts of sun, nutrients, and water depending on individual requirements; horticulturists are the first to admit that even flowers of the identical variety often require differing amounts of attention. So it is with gifted and talented children. They are all different and should be treated as individuals. To prescribe the same program for each of them simply because of a somewhat artificial label they have in common would be inappropriate. It is crucial that parents know about the field of gifted and talented education (see Chapter V for further information).

2. **Communicate with your child:** While learning about gifted and talented education in general is vital, it is perhaps even more important that parents learn about their own child's needs. The assessments used in identification can be useful in this sense, though there is nothing quite as revealing as when parents and child establish and maintain a high degree of openness in communication. In homes where parents and child communicate honestly and without fear of repercussion, parents are better informed about their child's needs. Where parents have encouraged the expression of wants, desires, fears, joys, needs, and an array of other feelings, the gifted and talented child is likely to keep the family

informed about the good and the bad encounters in life. Perhaps one of the best means for teaching children to communicate with you is for you to model the behavior by communicating your own feelings openly to them. While there is nothing wrong with maintaining an air of stoicism in some situations outside the home, such pretended or actual indifference to one's emotional life within the home itself is not healthy and will not allow for the growth of openness and honesty in communication.

3. **Become an accomplished listener:** Communication must include listening. Unfortunately, many people seem to forget this, and even when they remember to listen, they are so inexperienced at it that they do not listen well. Practice listening to each and every word your child says, remaining interested, caring, and nonjudgmental. Use acceptance signals such as leaning forward, nodding your head, smiling, and using lots of eye contact. If you and your child are communicating openly, there may be times when he or she may ask questions that you consider intrusive. A six-year-old who inquires about where he came from should be directed toward age-appropriate reading materials or engaged in a generalized discussion; this is not the time to teach the facts of life. In contrast, a young adolescent who asks the same type of question should be directed toward other reading materials, but must also be spoken to frankly and openly.

Regardless of age, rather than simply dismissing challenging questions, provide your child with some guidance as to why you would rather not respond at this time. Similarly, when you are asked questions that you cannot answer, openly admit it and assist your child in seeking other sources for answers. This approach is particularly useful with young children because you can begin teaching them where to locate answers to their own questions and how to go about using different resources. Moreover, as a good listener, it is probable that you will discern many clues about your child's interests. While it is

11

good to expose any child to a variety of books and magazines, museums, and historical sites, it is absolutely essential that the child select his or her own interests; if your child elects to pursue an interest to greater depths, encourage that, but never force your child to undertake *your* interests.

4. **Remember your child is a child:** Nearly every guide ever written for parents of gifted students includes a caution about treating the gifted child first as a child and second as gifted. Why? It is likely that this may be the most violated of all the tips for parents of gifted and talented children. The mother who cannot understand why her musically gifted seven-year-old son does not want to practice the piano every second of every day instead of permitting him to ride his bike has most definitely forgotten this tip. The father who forces his academically gifted 15-year-old daughter to read instead of allowing her some extended time to chat on the telephone has also forgotten.

The gifted and talented child will typically behave like most children of the same age in almost all respects. Not every statement or product will be profound or insightful, and questions may sometimes be no more intellectually perceptive than those any child poses. Most importantly, your child needs your *unconditional* love, guidance, and support. Furthermore, if there are other children in the family or within the neighborhood "family," *do not* compare your gifted child to them or vice-versa. Frankly, boasting about any child's exploits to family or friends only helps reinforce the stereotype of the gifted and talented child as a self-centered know-it-all. Even grandparents are eventually likely to tire of such braggadocio, and open boasting can nurture arrogance in the child as well. Remember, tight halos give everyone bad headaches.

5. **Don't be a "stage" parent:** Even if you are rearing the next Dorothy Hamill or George Washington Carver, do not expect your child to perform all of the time. Allow your gifted and talented child—as you would any child—time to stare

into space or simply play alone or with friends. These relaxation activities are very important; studies have shown that such activity allows people time to "incubate," or to think in detail about ideas, ultimately helping them become consciously aware of and gain skill in using their own thinking processes (known as "metacognition") (Feldman, 1988; Flavell, 1985; Sternberg, 1981). Such activities can also help spawn creativity because the child has had time to sort through a wide variety of options that can help enhance the number of ideas (fluency), the types of ideas (flexibility), the uniqueness of ideas (originality), and the details related to ideas (elaboration). A child who is occupied in play instead of working on a project, taking a dance lesson, or being involved in some other structured activity may be thinking about doing something very special.

All people, whether contemplating something creative or not, require "down" time that is unstructured. While parents should assist their children in scheduling time so that it is used wisely, too much structure and not enough free time can be detrimental. In today's busy, competitive world, it is not uncommon for parents of gifted children to resort to intensive over-structuring. Some bright children live the misfortune of leaving a tiring day at school only to march from one structured environment to another. Sadly, many of them will never complain because they believe they need to be involved in such experiences in order to please their parents.

6.   **Set clear and consistent expectations:** A system of consistency will not only help create an environment of integrity and ethics (not a bad example to set in and of itself), but it also will assist parents in enforcing discipline. Gifted children must be taught at home that they are not exempt from family or community rules. They must have your direction if they are to learn to share, and because they have a great deal to share, this aspect of parenting a gifted child may be the most important. Remember, your child's ability to share and

work with others will affect relationships in the family, school, and community; it also will be with your child the remainder of his or her life.

II. The School Bureaucracy:

How Does It Influence My Gifted Child?

Schools are social institutions that have been established with the expressed intent of educating our children. However, they are also bureaucracies in the sense that they tend to be complex organizations, often employing hundreds of professionals in various roles, all coordinated to achieve the highest degree of educational success within limitations imposed by time, finances, and space. While schools and school districts vary from place to place, there are some commonalties among them about which parents of a gifted and talented child must be knowledgeable if they want to optimize their child's educational opportunities.

Administration and Organization

Public school systems are governed by a board of education or school committee that, in most cases, is an elected body composed of citizens from the community it serves. Some school districts are governed by appointed school boards, which makes communication a little trickier. Regardless, a school superintendent usually is the individual charged with the responsibility of seeing that the school system operates as successfully as possible. While in most locations the superintendent is hired by an elected board, the superintendent of schools in some places is elected directly by the public.

Depending on the size of the school district, the superintendent may have ultimate day-to-day authority over all aspects of the school, from lunches to buses to curriculum to personnel; he or she may have a team of associate, assistant, or deputy superintendents or directors who see to the more mundane daily operation of the various components of schools. Generally, if the school system is large enough to require more than three or four school buildings, there will be a central administrative team of people (often referred to as the superintendent's "cabinet") who, one by one, undertake each of the specific features of the school program. For example, it is not unusual for the instructional component of schools to be directed by an associate superintendent, while yet another associate superintendent supervises finances, and yet another governs the physical plant; the larger the school district's student enrollment, the larger the central administrative team is likely to be.

In most school districts, principals or heads of schools serve as the school building-level administrators, and usually these are the parents' first link with the school system administration. In larger schools, there may be one or more associate or assistant principals or deans who work on some specific component of the school building. It is common, for instance, for assistant principals to handle the bulk of disciplinary issues, thus freeing the principal to supervise instruction. Keep in mind that, as schools developed historically in the United States, principals were the "master teachers" in their school buildings, or the teacher who was most able to demonstrate the best instruction and who acted as a role model for the other teachers. Hence, the history of education is partially responsible for school principals being charged with the guidance of curriculum and teaching at the building level. For parents of gifted and talented students who are often concerned about their child's opportunities, the principal, acting in his or her role as master teacher, is the first administrative contact should there be questions about instruction and curriculum beyond those that can be handled by the classroom teacher.

Teachers

Just as there are excellent and not-so excellent physicians and superior and inferior business executives, there are outstanding and inadequate teachers. Although there is a general tendency for school administrators to defend their teachers regardless of the differences in instructional abilities (it is part of their role as managers in the school system), parents need to remember that different individuals respond differently to different teaching styles. Consequently, it is appropriate for you to get to know your child's teacher, including the teacher's interests, strengths, and weaknesses. Would it not be a shame to have your son or daughter, who is highly interested and motivated in science, spend the year with a teacher who hates the subject? Meanwhile, across the hall, a teacher of the same grade level has a major in science and emphasizes scientific thinking in her teaching. Such poor decisions in placement of children are common, but for parents of gifted and talented children, these placement errors could mean special trouble.

Ideally, schools should examine the match between students and teachers prior to placement. This would help greatly in alleviating conflicts related to interests and teaching/learning styles, issues that are especially of concern for gifted and talented students. However, in most schools, placement is often a task that is not as well thought out as it should be; in fact, some schools truly place children with teachers at random in an effort to insure heterogeneity (a mixture of children of all types of abilities and needs), a reflection of the "real world" in which children will have to function as adults. Sadly, a number of schools take heterogeneous placement to mean that teachers and students must "put up" with each other at the cost of interests and teaching/learning styles. Unlike the school's view of the "real world," adults are inclined to affiliate with people who appreciate more or less the same things and operate in more or less the same ways. While adults certainly work and associate with a heterogeneous group of people, most adults tend to select others who are similar as friends and work partners.

Stereotypes often affect teachers' behavior toward different sorts of students (Anyon, 1987; Wilcox, 1982). For the parents of a child who has been labeled gifted, a term that is entrenched in stereotypes, the problem could become severe (Renzulli, 1994). For example, a teacher who does not particularly appreciate your child's interests or learning preferences may expect that, because of giftedness, your child can quickly adjust to whatever the topic or teaching strategies the teacher has selected. In addition, a teacher who accepts traditional yet unwarranted beliefs about gifted and talented students could expect your child to excel equally well in all subjects, and could perhaps become impatient when your child encounters difficulties with some tasks. Even worse, such a teacher might overlook your child when he or she legitimately needs additional practice on a concept or skill.

The classroom teacher is the most important adult in terms of your child's education. It is imperative that your child be placed with a teacher who is sufficiently open-minded to meet your son or daughter's educational needs without defining your child's identity by using an imagined stereotype. Furthermore, your child's interests and learning preferences must be ones that the teacher can willingly address. To say that every teacher is perfect for every child is as ridiculous as pretending there is no need for specialization in medicine. If your child's school attempts to match teachers and students on interests and styles, then you will have little need for becoming involved. However, if yours is like the majority of schools, you will need to have knowledge of the teachers in advance of placement. Generally, most school principals are willing to acknowledge parental desires so long as the case is presented appropriately: based on facts and without anger.

How to Communicate Effectively with School Administrators and Teachers

Because of their children's particular educational needs, parents of gifted students must be prepared to establish the same type of open and honest communication with school officials as with their children. If parents establish rapport with the school administration and teachers that is honest and not founded on hostility, chances are good that parents will be able to play a significant and helpful role in enhancing their child's school program. The old adage about "catching flies with honey" definitely pertains.

First and foremost, schools, like all other bureaucracies, want parents to follow the chain of command. For a parent to approach the superintendent about his or her child without first pursuing dialog with others at the school building level is unacceptable. A parent's first communication link with school officials is through the classroom teacher. The way in which parents approach teachers can have a profound influence on the outcomes of communication. It will prove advantageous to good communication if you make an appointment with the teacher early in the school year.

Send a short note requesting a meeting, making certain to convey exactly what it is you would like to discuss; initial meetings of this type are helpful forums in which to introduce yourself and the details you would like to relate to the teacher about your child. Therefore, your note requesting an initial

19

meeting should state that you would like to meet as a means for getting better acquainted and that you would like to offer some assistance. Be prepared to offer the teacher your time for some class project, like chaperoning a field trip or hosting the class at your place of business, or express a desire to assist in some on-going way, like serving as a room parent or voluntarily working one-to-one with a student who may need a little extra attention. It takes a lot of effort to teach school, and any volunteers are generally appreciated.

Once you have introduced yourself and expressed an interest in providing the classroom with some assistance, the teacher is more likely to value you as a contact. It will then be relatively easy to move the conversation to your own child, what giftedness means for him or her, and what types of interests he or she has. If you have been genuine in your introduction and offers of assistance, the teacher, in the vast majority of cases, will be eager to hear what you have to say and will not interpret your remarks defensively. It will be important for you to practice astute listening when you meet with the teacher and to make certain your approach is characterized by a team spirit: that "we're all in this year with my child *together*." However, should you wait to schedule your first meeting later in the school year or after there have been some problems for your child, this approach will not be successful. This strategy is only helpful if scheduled very early in your child's association with the teacher.

If you fail to establish an early working relationship with the teacher, you should request a meeting in writing and explain in the note exactly what has suddenly prompted you to desire such personal communication. Perhaps it is simply a case that you were preoccupied with other tasks and were unable to find time to request a meeting; if that is the case, state so. In all likelihood, if you state your request honestly, the teacher will be as accepting as if you had arranged an early-in-the-year meeting. Again, it is recommended that you offer assistance of some type, even if it is only volunteering to bake cupcakes or make popcorn for an upcoming classroom celebration.

In the event you have waited to schedule your first meeting after your child has experienced some problem in school, you will need to approach the teacher in some other way. Honesty still is best; a short note requesting the meeting and explaining the exact nature of your concern will usually not put the teacher on the defensive, particularly if you indicate that you want to work *with* him or her to resolve the difficulty. It may also help if you indicate that there is some information you would like to share about your child's home and out-of-school life that may be influencing school. Even if the information you supply is simply to explain that your child has not been getting sufficient sleep due to a busy schedule, it may be sufficient to make the teacher comfortable enough so that your discussion can focus on whatever the actual issue may be.

It is always helpful if you offer to provide the teacher with additional information about your child, particularly about his or her gifts and talents. While the teacher will have access to the school assessment information, he or she may not have any idea about your child's leisure activities and interests. The majority of teachers want to know these things because student interests frequently can be used to enhance instruction. Although you never want to indicate in any way that the teacher does not know how to teach gifted students, it can be useful if you offer to share some interesting articles or materials about working with gifted students. Do this with care, in the spirit of teamwork, so as not to offend the teacher.

If communication with the teacher fails for some reason, or your child's educational needs are not adequately met despite continual communication with the teacher, your next communication with the school should probably be through the principal or his or her appointee, such as an assistant principal or school counselor. Again, it will not harm your position to send a written request and, at the same time, extend some offer that is likely both to enhance your child's education and prove beneficial to the school overall.

Remember, however, that once you progress beyond the teacher, it is probable that your relationship with him or her will never be as amicable again. In addition, you may possibly be viewed as a "pushy parent" by teachers and administration alike. It truly is in everyone's best interests for the parent to be *proactive*—to make sure the teacher with whom your child is placed shares some interests and preferences in common with the child—and to make early and on-going communication with the school a family priority. For parents to be *reactive*— to wait to communicate either late in the year or only after there are problems—is likely to jeopardize the school experience for your child for that particular school year. If parents make a point to indicate to the teacher their interest in forming a cooperative effort between home and school, the entire school year is more likely to be one in which the gifted child flourishes.

III. School Gifted Programs:

What They Are and How Parents Can Ensure Success

There are literally hundreds of different approaches and instructional techniques that are used in gifted programs today. The majority of public school programs for gifted and talented students can be grouped around either one or a combination of two popular philosophies: acceleration and enrichment. It is relatively rare to find programs that are completely of either type to the exclusion of the other. School gifted programs usually will combine characteristics of each of these types of programs.

The Acceleration Type

Acceleration programs are based on advancing students "through skills and/or content at their own pace, moving through the basic educational sequence at a rate suitable to their abilities" (Swassing, 1985, p. 11). This type of program not only permits but encourages students to study new material that is normally taught at a higher grade level than the one in which the child is currently enrolled. It also encourages them to be involved in instruction that has been hurried to cover more material in a shorter time.

Included in the concept of acceleration are any activities that serve to move the student more rapidly through school and the school curriculum. A youngster who completes grade three and skips over grade four into the fifth grade has experienced *acceleration by grade level*. Similarly, the child who completes eighth-grade algebra while enrolled in sixth grade, or the student who has condensed a one-year biology class into one semester, are examples of *acceleration by content*. The assumption underlying acceleration programs is that gifted and talented children are probably achieving at advanced levels of skill and should, therefore, be studying new material at levels that are commensurate with their abilities. The acceleration philosophy can be applied to any single area or all academic areas or to a single talent/non-academic area. Children can be accelerated in all school subjects or in only one based on their particular abilities. Likewise, children who are talented in art, writing, music, or athletics can also be accelerated; in the talent areas, in fact, acceleration is more common. Examples include art and music students and athletically gifted young people who typically move along at their own pace in developing their abilities.

Because acceleration programs have been in use for many years in serving the needs of gifted students, there is a great deal of research supporting them. Studies about acceleration programs and their effects on participating students have been almost uniformly positive, though studies have largely concentrated on mathematical and foreign language abilities without consideration for other areas (Keating, 1976; Kulik & Kulik, 1991; Stanley et al., 1974; VanTassel-Baska, 1981). In studies of mathematically accelerated students, it has been suggested that they have not been stifled by boredom and that their fondness for math and their abilities to think mathematically have been enhanced (Benbow, 1986; Stanley & Benbow, 1983, 1986).

The Enrichment Type

Enrichment programs, in contrast, concentrate on learning through activities that broaden the range of experiences and topics addressed by the basic school program. Such experiences might include guest speakers, field trips, specialized meetings and projects, and other kinds of events aimed at providing young people with access to information not ordinarily covered by the regular school curriculum. Enrichment, at least to some degree, is generally appropriate for all students, but for gifted and talented students, these enrichment experiences serve as foundations for further, more advanced exploration of the topics. The purpose of enrichment programs is to stimulate gifted and talented children to pursue in-depth study in areas of interest and to develop their abilities in those areas. The nature of in-depth study means that these students will become involved in the complex ideas and concepts related to a topic, will learn the appropriate methods and techniques for doing first-hand investigative work on the topic, and will spend large amounts of time in advanced thinking skills (applying, analyzing, synthesizing, and evaluating aspects of the topic) related to the interest area.

For example, in an enrichment-based gifted and talented program, it would not be unusual for a fourth-grader to be exposed to a wide variety of information through special speakers, films, exploration of artifacts and tools, and field activities related to the field of archaeology. If the interest in the topic continued, the child would learn the various adult-level techniques used by actual archaeologists and would be both permitted and encouraged to pursue some kind of original archaeological investigation. The child might pursue a real-life archaeological dig, including analysis of the artifacts found and a report of the findings, which could be presented by the child to the local historical society.

Unlike acceleration programs, the enrichment type programs rely much more heavily on the notion of assisting children in the identification of areas of interest and subsequently helping them develop those interests. The ultimate goal of enrichment programs for gifted students is to expose children to the many subjects and opportunities available in the world and then to encourage their pursuit of one or more of them to a high degree of sophistication. Enrichment programs also frequently incorporate some focus on the individual child's social and emotional needs because it is believed that, in order to pursue an area of interest to an in-depth level, certain kinds of social and emotional skills (e.g., setting of goals, managing stress and time, and working with others) must be on solid footing.

Although not as plentiful as the research on acceleration due to its relative youth as a program structure, research supporting the enrichment program type is growing as quickly as the numbers of schools that are employing such programs with gifted and talented students. However, like the studies in acceleration, the results have been quite uniformly positive. Gifted and talented students involved in enrichment programs are likely to become producers of new ideas and products outside of school (Schack, 1986; Starko, 1986), to view school learning as a means to an end as opposed to an end itself (Olenchak, 1988, 1990, 1994), to enjoy learning both in and out of traditional school settings (Olenchak & Renzulli, 1989), and to have a better understanding of the world (Gallagher, 1985).

Combinations of Enrichment and Acceleration

In real practice, few gifted and talented programs adhere strictly to either an acceleration or an enrichment design. Rather, by considering the interests, learning styles, and social/emotional needs of each child as an individual, most gifted programs will develop an approach of their own that is based on a combination of practices in order to meet the needs of the students enrolled. For most highly able students, a "combination of approaches is most practical and necessary as a means for satisfying student needs" (Clark, 1988, p. 215). Frankly, most schools are less troubled than researchers about the apparent differences between the philosophies of acceleration and enrichment so long as students can be served adequately.

It must be noted that two extremely popular program models that have been widely used by schools nationwide and around the world, the SMPY (Study of Mathematically Precocious Youth) and the SEM (Schoolwide Enrichment Model), both include aspects of acceleration and enrichment. Despite the fact that SMPY is viewed primarily as an acceleration program, it entails a mentorship in which children work directly with practicing mathematicians who, by virtue of their mentoring roles, expose or *enrich* students in mathematics. SEM, primarily an enrichment programming framework, includes a component for "compacting," or reducing the amount of time students spend on school material they have already mastered, so that time is created in school for gifted and talented students to work on their individual interest areas and to *accelerate* in subjects where appropriate.

Program Delivery Options

Beyond the programming philosophy, schools have a wide range of options as to how services will be delivered to students in the gifted and talented program. Whether of an enrichment, acceleration, or combination type, programs can use a number of different administrative designs to work with students within the limits imposed by a traditional school schedule. Some of the more popular options are listed in Table 2 on page 87, along with related advantages and disadvantages of each.

What Parents Can Do to Monitor the Program

There are a number of things parents can do to make certain the program in which their child is involved is appropriate. These activities, for the most part, require only a little extra effort and time. However, they can make a great difference between a program that is successful for your child and one that is either mediocre or poor. Activities in which parents can engage are of two types: direct and indirect.

Direct Activities

When parents can become directly involved in school programs for the gifted and talented, they are then able to monitor those programs from perhaps the most ideal vantage point. Direct activities are those in which parents are engaged with the program on some regular basis. Whether daily, weekly, monthly, or even annually, parents involved in this way are afforded an opportunity to examine how the program has been designed and the ways in which it is likely to benefit children in general and enhance their own child's education in particular. This kind of volunteerism means that parents will need to work directly with the program's students and teachers in some manner. The most common type of direct activity is that of teaching. Many successful programs for gifted students regularly involve parents as teachers in a way that allows them to share areas of expertise with groups of students or with individuals. In either event, parents should be prepared to offer information and ideas regarding their areas of expertise in a manner that is appropriate for the students involved. The program teacher should be willing to advise parents so that their work with children is appropriate to age and degree of interest.

Before agreeing to serve the program in this way, make sure you have assessed your abilities to present your material effectively and in a manner that is exciting to your intended audience. Remember that lecture you once attended that was delivered by a renowned expert in art, chemistry, politics, or scuba diving? Do you also recall that you were bored and unmotivated by the event? There simply is no reason to believe that expertise in a field guarantees teaching ability, and this point is especially important to recall when working with children who are searching and exploring new topics or are attempting to learn more about old ones.

This kind of involvement can be scheduled as a one-time presentation, but usually there is need for additional follow-up sessions. Certainly, if parents are to employ the direct involvement approach, contact should be scheduled more frequently than one time. To a large degree, however, additional work with students should be determined by the students themselves in high quality gifted and talented programs.

An excellent technique that allows parents a direct and ongoing relationship with the gifted program and, at the same time, provides an outstanding opportunity to one student or to a small group is that of mentoring. However, whether or not you serve as a mentor should be dictated by the desires of one or more students who want to pursue your area of expertise to a degree that is not of particular interest to other students. The significance of the mentor role on personal and vocational development is clearly documented in research regarding highly successful persons (Bloom, 1982, 1985; Goertzel & Goertzel, 1962; Simonton, 1984).

Mentors often serve many needs at once. These include those related to personality growth, counseling, and teaching skills. Perhaps more than any other, the mentor role means modeling of behavior that is characteristic of successful thinking and action in the particular area of expertise. In this sense, it is entirely possible for parents to serve as mentors to their own children, though there is sufficient documentation that such parent-child mentorships are difficult and can prompt difficult family rapport (Goertzel & Goertzel, 1962). Generally, most schools probably frown on parent-child mentorships because of a belief, right or wrong, that such mentoring can take place in the home and that school should expose students to others. However, if one's own child shares a com-

29

mon interest, there is no reason why a parent-child mentorship cannot be extremely beneficial educationally.

Direct involvement can also mean that parents never work directly with the students in the program; instead, they work with the program staff. This type of involvement can afford as many or perhaps even greater opportunities for parents to monitor the program's provisions for their own children. Activities of this kind include organizing human and material resources, making contacts with guest presenters and arranging their work with the students, pursuing field trip possibilities, and generally serving the program instructors as assistants. Being included in discussions about the design and implementation of program activities can truly permit parents an "inside-out" perspective, seeing the program from its planning roots through to its concluding evaluations.

Indirect Activities

While direct activities may take more time and energy, indirect involvement is more difficult. It is easy for busy parents to become preoccupied with the many demands of daily life and overlook the gifted program. It is this preoccupation that can lead a bright child to begin viewing the gifted and talented program as unimportant. A gifted and talented program of quality is not a lark, having been formulated purposefully to enhance the growth and development of those students participating in it. Moreover, if a child has been recommended for placement in the program, it was obviously felt that the program would be useful to that individual. When parents fail to convey the program's importance to their children, it is not unusual for those young people to view the program as extraneous. Gifted program rolls nationwide are filled with names of students who have dropped out of the program.

The reasons for students leaving gifted programs are too numerous to mention, but they can be grouped as those attributable to the child, those related to the program, and those connected to parents. Those related to the child include social and emotional issues like failure to handle peer pressure. One middle school-aged girl elaborated:

> I just couldn't figure why I needed to be in that program when I have lots of friends who are more popular than I am. They wonder why I spend my time in the program, and I guess I began wondering, too. It is very important to me to keep my friends, and being too different from them is no way to strengthen my ties with them. I decided that being in the program made me just too different and could really make me an outcast. High school is just a year away, and I'd like to be popular.

Similarly, when a child declines involvement in a gifted and talented program due to either the program itself or to parental attitudes, the child has come to believe, for whatever reason, that not participating in the program will be more beneficial than being involved. More than not, such a decision is rooted in peer pressure, the primary reason some gifted students decide not to participate in special programs. Parents can and must fight against such pressure. Two primary strategies are recommended.

First, through open lines of communication with the school, parents should notify the administration and teachers associated with the gifted program that peer pressure has become a concern. Schools can, in fact, do a great deal to create a positive atmosphere for gifted and talented education; paralleling athletic award ceremonies that are so prevalent in schools, assemblies in which talent *of all kinds* is acknowledged and rewarded can enhance other activities in which teachers show students the valuable contributions to society made by people in all walks of life. Parents can assist schools with such undertakings by helping to arrange guest appearances and also serving as watchdogs to make sure maximal involvement is promoted for *all* children in every field of human performance. Some of the very children who may make your academically talented child feel as if he or she is weird are those who may excel in some domain other than the academic realm.

Second, parents must undertake early with their own gifted child an appreciation of the full range of the vocations and avocations that make life better for everyone. A child who has been reared in a home where all kinds of human contributions are revered is likely to be slow to yield to anti-gifted peer pressure. Moreover, such a child is more likely to have a open mind regarding the array of professions and hobbies available in life.

Ultimately, it is the responsibility of parents to oversee their children, and parental intervention can be a major influence on whether or not children are productive in school, including gifted programs. For example, the parents of the middle schooler quoted earlier obviously have neglected to bolster her self-concept sufficiently to allow her to maintain friendships outside of the gifted program while she participates in it. Her self-perception, like that of most adolescents, is defined by her peers. However, she has not been helped to see that her non-gifted program friends are not really friends at all if they cannot accept her for who she is: a gifted student.

With respect to the program itself, parents who are indirectly involved, must make certain that the program contains the components of successful gifted and talented educational offerings. The more of these components a program includes, the better the program is likely to be. These components include:

◆ evidence of a plan that provides continuity through each grade level and between grade levels explaining the goals and objectives to be attained;

◆ an individual held accountable for coordination of the

program on at least the school level, if not system-wide as well;

♦ a continuous program of in-service training for school personnel and parents;

♦ utilization of multiple criteria for identification purposes so that program involvement is not based simply on a single test score or single recommendation;

♦ specialized consideration for children who are economically or culturally disadvantaged or who present other kinds of special needs in addition to their potential giftedness;

♦ curriculum and instructional techniques corresponding with individual student's learning styles, abilities, needs, and interests;

♦ presence of at least one program teacher with whom each child seems to relate through playful, hands-on, interest-based learning experiences who, at the same time, instills an appreciation for excellence in the student;

♦ flexibility in program content, pace, and schedule that acknowledges the individual learning needs of each child;

♦ evidence that many people are involved in the program, including teachers as well as parents and persons from the community at large; and

♦ presence of at least one professional who is willing to serve as the child's school advocate, intervening as needed with teachers outside the program.

Finally, parents themselves, through their attitudes and behavior, can serve to monitor the gifted program in which their children are enrolled. Taking time to find out exactly what the program is all about, learning who the teachers are not only by name but as people, and taking an interest in a child's program activities all convey to the child that the program is important. Busy or not so busy, parents can monitor the gifted program by staying abreast of it and of their own child's pursuits related to it. Indirect roles do not require parents to do anything more than monitor the gifted program

33

and their child's activities in school.

What If There's No Formal Program?
What Parents Can Do

There is a great deal of research underscoring the need for specialized programs for gifted students and documenting benefits of such programs (Benbow, 1986; Clark, 1988; Reis et al., 1993; Renzulli, 1994). In the event there are no formalized gifted programs available, the parental responsibility to secure appropriate educational attention is heightened.

First, parents must establish a working relationship with their child's teachers. It is imperative that parents not place teachers on the defensive with prolonged discussions about how gifted and talented the child is. Rather, parents, in a matter-of-fact fashion, should explain to teachers that the child has been identified as having some particular learning needs and then strive to describe *both* the child's strengths and weaknesses. Nothing can be more offensive to others than to listen to parents' lengthy descriptions of their child's various feats. Make certain teachers are aware that, while the weaknesses demand treatment, so do the strengths; competent teachers will fully understand you when you plead for more time to be spent on strengths than on weaknesses. At the same time, offer your services to teachers as a support, explaining that assistance will be provided at home as needed or requested, and express your willingness to volunteer within the school as room parent or other assistant. Parents who clearly present themselves to teachers as cooperative and well-meaning most often come away with appropriate attention for their child in school. A more thorough discussion of the possibilities for parents regarding "regular" classrooms is provided in the following chapter of this text.

Second, establish a working relationship with school

34

administrators. Show your support of the school and its mission by attending parent-teacher association meetings, volunteering to assist with schoolwide activities and fund-raisers, and occasionally visiting the school. In other words, let the administration know who you are by name. Even the busiest of parents can sometimes squeeze time to become known at the school in a positive, not pesky sense. Perhaps parents can assist with printing some school newsletters or making telephone calls to other parents. As one very successful father put it: "I am swamped most of the time, but I can always find a little time to visit the school for lunch with my daughter or to call the principal to see if I can help out in some way." Parents who are known to be *actively* supportive of administration are more likely to secure appropriate attention for their children in school. Furthermore, should school problems develop for their children, parents who carry positive school reputations are most likely to secure quick resolutions from the administration.

Third, if parents are ultimately interested in seeing that a gifted and talented program is developed in the school, they can openly discuss this interest with teachers and administrators if cooperative communication has been established beforehand. Pursuing development of a new gifted program is no small task, and parents who elect to do so will require as much support from schools as possible. In addition, parents who decide to pursue a program where one has not been in existence should contact their state department of education as well as state and local representatives of parent and professional associations for the gifted and talented (see Chapter VI).

Finally, if all else has failed—teachers will not work with you, administrators avoid you, and there is little hope for developing a new gifted program—become involved at the school system level. Obtain the goals and objectives of the school district; nearly all school systems maintain goals that speak to the individual learning needs of *every* student. Meet with the superintendent of schools to discuss your interest in establishing a gifted and talented program, and make sure to ask how to go about securing such programming. Organize a group of parents and community members who are interested in the prospects of gifted education, regularly attend the school board meetings, and let your group's interests be known. Most of all, parents, as they engage in the lengthy process of school change, must not forget their child's educational needs. Only after you have made every positive attempt to work cooperatively with the school in order to provide for your child's needs should you seek a change in teachers or even in schools.

IV. Regular Classrooms:

Can Anything Be Done There?

Whether or not there are specialized program provisions for gifted and talented students, every school-aged child spends time in a regular classroom. In this sense, *regular* encompasses the classroom setting in which students spend the majority of their time engaged in activities that may not directly account for individual learning preferences. In a typical school, the regular classroom is that in which students, either heterogeneously or homogeneously grouped, spend time with teachers covering a predesignated curriculum with few opportunities for individually tailored instruction. Even in magnet schools for gifted and talented children, in which students are often hand-selected for participation, a regular classroom atmosphere frequently prevails during at least a portion of each school day.

Since gifted and talented children spend a large portion of their school time in regular classrooms, it is both appropriate and necessary for teachers in regular classes to accommodate the particular learning needs of these students. While this seems logical and sounds easy, it is not always a simple task to secure the kinds of attention in regular classrooms that are likely to benefit your child. In fact, many teachers believe gifted and talented students should be able to make it on their own without special educational accommodations, and some teachers even resent or are suspect of the gifted student's special abilities. Therefore, it is not always easy for parents to ensure appropriate classroom treatment for their children.

Where schools have undertaken on-going staff development through in-service workshops in gifted education, it is probable that parents will have less convincing to do. Even in locales in which a commitment to school personnel development in gifted education does not exist, parents still have support for their cause. Nearly all schools and school districts in the United States maintain mission statements pertaining to the adequate educational service of *all* students. These statements of school policy, whether or not there are specialized gifted programs and receptive teachers, legally mean the schools must strive to accommodate the educational needs of gifted and talented students as appropriately as possible. However, these policies do not mean that the schools are in any way obligated to tailor an individualized program as dictated by your child's needs, except in school systems and states in which such has been mandated by statutory action (a detailed explanation is provided in Chapter I).

It is imperative that parents approach the school situation delicately; the strategies outlined in Chapter II are recommended because they have a history of success. In addition, the discussions in Chapter III will prove helpful in working cooperatively with the school and the teacher. However, there are some specific accommodations teachers can provide, even in the absence of a formal gifted program, which parents of gifted and talented children should seek in their child's classroom.

Curriculum Compacting or Streamlining

One of the most basic accommodations that teachers can provide for gifted and talented youngsters in the regular classroom is reduction of the amount of time and energy spent on material the children already know. Termed "curriculum compacting" (Reis, Burns, & Renzulli, 1992; Renzulli, Smith, & Reis, 1982), such instructional adjustment sounds sensible, but it must never be assumed that classrooms make this kind of accommodation as a matter of course. Previous studies of regular classrooms, their methods, and their materials have revealed that compacting of basic skills curricula is not a customary practice because teachers tend to teach whole groups of students with little or no variation for individual student needs (Cuban, 1982; Goodlad, 1983; Olenchak, 1991; Reis et al., 1993). Moreover, there is reason to believe that, because of the overall decline in textbook difficulty, much of the material addressed in regular classrooms may be at levels that are largely inadequate to stimulate or challenge gifted and talented students (Bernstein, 1985; Chall & Conrad, 1991; Educational Products Information Exchange Institute, 1981; Kirst, 1982; Taylor & Frye, 1988). Therefore, due to the persistence of whole-group instruction and a reliance on textbooks for determining what the curricula will be, curriculum compacting is vital for gifted students in the regular classroom setting.

Curriculum compacting, or streamlining the basic curriculum, is a proven strategy in which classroom teachers first examine each student for his or her strengths. This is in stark contrast to the "find-it-fix-it" mentality that steers most schools, as school personnel customarily spend literally hours searching for student weaknesses so they can be remediated up to some level of acceptability. By focusing on students' strengths, teachers can review previous grades and tests, current levels of performance, and interests in order to form some initial ideas about areas in which children might be expected to perform well.

For instance, if sixth-grader Lawrie Beth has made 100% on her spelling tests year after year, it could accurately be concluded that she is likely to require less time in spelling than needed by most other students in her regular classroom.

Similarly, if she scored in the 95th percentile or higher each year on the school's standardized mathematics tests, it would make sense that she may be able to spend less time on basic math concepts and could move a bit faster than her age peers *even if she has not secured straight A's in her previous school performance.* Keep in mind that if one feels disinterested in mundane tasks because of a seemingly unending series of workbook exercises of the same type, it is quite likely that the student will not bother to exert great effort to achieve perfect grades. In both cases, teachers who are familiar with curriculum reduction techniques would, at the very least, be likely to keep a watchful eye over Lawrie Beth in spelling and mathematics to make sure she is taught at an appropriate level and pace.

At approximately the same time the teacher studies students for possible areas of strength, he or she will determine the level of accuracy necessary for mastery of a particular set of concepts, skills, or information. For example, it has been decided by professionals that children must master their alphabet at the 100% level in order to function successfully later in both reading and writing. On the other hand, 100% memory of each of the chemical symbols from the Periodic Table of Elements may not be appropriate, given that one can reference the Periodic Table at any point to ascertain the symbols of elements. In this situation, perhaps professionals might determine that mastery of the chemical symbols from memory is adequate at 85%.

The classroom teacher then sets about assessing students' needs on an individual basis; sometimes this is best accomplished through pretesting—testing concepts and skills before they have been taught. The teacher may elect to measure every student in this manner, or only those whom she suspects can demonstrate mastery of the material before classroom coverage. Because many teachers systematically use pretesting as a means for finding students who are likely to require extra assistance (i.e., finding their *weaknesses*), this approach should not seem foreign to most teachers. In addition to pretesting, teachers can form a view of a student's knowledge through classroom discussions, conversations with parents and other teachers, and conscious observation of the child's progress in texts and classroom activities. During this phase, teachers may uncover needed skills or information while also developing rapid ways for filling in any "holes" in a child's knowledge. However, if a child has demonstrated a thorough knowledge of fractions except for the concept of lowest common factor, it should not take very long for the student to obtain total mastery in fractional mathematics.

Alert teachers who have been acclimated to curriculum compacting will take the lead in determining compacting needs in ways other than those related to the results of formal tests. Once, when a first-grade teacher was showing her class an introductory basic film about dinosaurs, a boy named Michael interrupted her with a question about the difference in "skeletal construction of carnivorous and herbivorous dinosaurs" and whether or not she thought "hadrosaurs were at the bottom of the chain because they didn't have a way to defend themselves against carnivores." Clearly, based on Michael's use of advanced terms and on the nature of his questions, he was not in need of a basic film about the dinosaur world. Fortunately for Michael, his teacher recognized this and worked with him and his gifted program teacher. Instead of spending time learning basic concepts about various dinosaurs, Michael spent school time developing and producing a handbook and accompanying videotape about dinosaurs that is still in use in that school some 15 years later.

It is this last part of curriculum compacting where parents can also be helpful. Certainly, parental input is helpful as teachers assess students' strengths. Parental advice may be especially helpful as teachers work with students to ensure that compacted classroom time is spent in fruitful ways; compacted time can be devoted to any number of enrichment projects, accelerated curriculum, or a combination of both. Parents are likely to know their children better than anyone and can provide information that may be useful to teachers. Returning to Michael's case, it was his father who reported to the teacher that Michael had been spending lots of time learning how videocameras worked. Michael's teachers used that information to benefit the child by guiding Michael's interests in dinosaurs in a way that accounted for who he was at the time: a young boy who was capable of learning more about two areas of interest—dinosaurs and videocameras. This turned out to be a highly beneficial and defensible use of compacted school time.

As with all other areas of gifted and talented education, parents must serve as watchdogs, making certain that the school accommodates the needs of their children in a manner that is appropriate. However, just as watchdogs must walk gently and gauge whether or not an attack is necessary, parents must learn to work cooperatively with teachers to instigate compacting in classrooms. The strategy, while logical and easy, is not one with which most teachers are familiar, and it is one about which few university undergraduate and graduate teacher preparatory programs make their trainees aware.

Counseling for Success

While it is improbable that most classroom teachers are certified counselors, most teachers have been trained to account for student social and emotional needs in the classroom. One of the most important means for curbing possible underachievement among gifted youth is for teachers and parents, working in tandem, to convey positive expectations to gifted children at all times—*even when the children are not performing up to expectations* (Jackson, Cleveland, & Mirenda, 1975; Bloom, 1985).

Parents must be prepared to provide cues to teachers regarding their children's social and emotional needs. It is generally accepted that, without a healthy outlook, even the most gifted child will be unlikely to succeed. Parental information can provide teachers with advanced warning that children are experiencing traumas at home or with peers. Effective parents and teachers are in constant communication, especially where student social and emotional needs are concerned. Even where classrooms are devoid of specific opportunities targeted for gifted students, an effective teacher-parent relationship can help make the experience a success.

Sarah's regular classroom teacher made it perfectly clear that no particular accommodations would be made for her because the school maintained a gifted program and "she could be gifted then." Sarah's parents could have given up or could have attacked the teacher. Instead, they increased communication about Sarah's academic, social, and emotional needs and made a point to contact the teacher regarding their daughter's state-of-mind at least once weekly. The contacts were always positive in nature and were clearly intended to "let the teacher know" about something that might have classroom performance ramifications. As the school year waned, the parents found that the teacher had never made special academic accommodations for Sarah, but Sarah liked the teacher nonetheless because "she cares about how I feel and is always there when I need somebody to give me a boost with the other kids or with my work."

This is an illustration of parents who, through positive communication, conveyed a message loudly and clearly to the teacher: they care about their child and want the teacher to help her get through the school part of life. Most teachers of any worth will respond to such parents, particularly when the communication is aimed at the child's social and emotional needs. While the fact that Sarah's teacher was unwilling to acknowledge her academic needs demonstrates a serious staff development void in the school, one child's parents alone are not likely to alter that. Sarah's parents concentrated their efforts on their own child's social and emotional development, and it paid off with a happy child. While she may have had to spend a great deal of class time on material she already knew, Sarah grew emotionally that year.

The fact that gifted and talented children are different from others in terms of social and emotional development is well documented (Delisle, 1992). As a result, it is entirely appropriate for gifted programs to provide counseling and other support components on both a preventative and remedial basis. When the needs of gifted children are ignored or go underserved, a variety of negative social and emotional behaviors can develop; some of the more serious include eating disorders and other self-destructive syndromes. For instance, a number of potentially disastrous behaviors among gifted youth have been avoided through open group seminars in which gifted students, in a protected environment, feel safe in sharing some of their feelings with a trained professional (Olenchak, 1994). Consequently, it is critical that parents make sure counseling is meaningfully incorporated into the gifted program.

Getting the Teacher to Owe You

Volunteerism has been discussed at length earlier in this book, but it may help to emphasize the point again. When parents are available as resources to teachers, it is quite likely that the degree of communication necessary for establishing curriculum compacting or for heightening a teacher's awareness of a child's social and emotional needs will already exist.

Cooperative volunteer work with a regular teacher could lead parents to act as liaisons between the classroom and the established gifted program. On more than one occasion, it has been parents who have facilitated working relationships between regular teachers and gifted program personnel. Furthermore, it is far easier to make requests of someone for whom you have previously done a favor, and this includes teachers. It is a common rule of thumb in life that "if you scratch my back, I'll scratch yours." The same goes for parents as they attempt to ensure programming of high quality for their gifted children.

V. Time for Action:

It's More Than Luck and a Prayer!

Although this book has offered a number of varied ways in which parents can work actively toward ensuring good school programming accommodations for their gifted and talented children, the common aspect among all of them is *action*. Parents cannot expect or anticipate that schools will automatically seek out and develop a high quality program for their gifted and talented child. While public schools tend to perform quite well at the task society has handed them (that of educating and socializing the masses of school-aged children from every background imaginable), few can dispute the fact that schools simply do not have the finances, staffing, materials, or time to examine the needs of each child individually. Certainly schools must do so for children whose needs are addressed by federal laws mandating such personalized treatment, but gifted and talented students are not included in the special education population nationwide. Hence, for parents of these children, responsibility for netting and maintaining an appropriate education is home-based; even where states have mandated school services for gifted children, parents must be cautious about this responsibility. As one mother from such a state commented: "I was told by the principal himself that they were doing what they could and that it was sufficient to meet state laws and that if I wasn't satisfied, perhaps I should send my child to a private school."

Appropriate Action

Parents can embark on a plan for guaranteeing good programming for their children without having to resort to alternative education or to argumentation. A summary of three roles most helpful for securing good programs for gifted and talented children includes:

1.   **Learn what is required and what is not.** Parents who take the time to know the definitions and approaches used in the field invariably help their children. How can you ask if you don't know what to ask for? It is worth the time to determine the rules and regulations in your school district, state, or province and work accordingly. As was mentioned earlier, nearly every school system in the United States maintains board of education policy advocating an educational process that enhances each *individual* child's growth and development. Consequently, in the event there are no specific services defined for gifted students, parents can, at the very least, turn to such board policies for support in their quest for appropriate programming. Knowledgeable parents understand not only the program options but also the rules that guide them. The existence of specific program provisions for educating the gifted and talented aside, it is always a parental responsibility to seek good education for their children.

2.   **Learn how to negotiate school bureaucracies and forge ahead.** Learning what is required by schools is only part of the task. The other part—working within the school structural framework—is just as important. The last thing a parent in search of appropriate schooling should do is offend school personnel by violating the chains of command. Parents must always begin their communications and inquiries with the personnel closest to their child's classroom program and move progressively further away from the instructional level if necessary. To do otherwise could brand a parent as a trou-

blemaker and seriously limit available options for securing the desired services.

3. **Learn how to communicate effectively.** Communication is the single most important tool in negotiating. Parents would be well advised to become the most effective communicators possible, including written and oral language. Moreover, communication is crucial not only between parent and school but also between parent and child. It is amazing the number of parents who are able to employ successful communication in their business lives but who become inept with their own children or with the school. One parent summarized it best: "My business is communication, but for some reason, I just do not handle my children or their school with the same candor I do my clients." Parents must learn to address their children and the school with clarity and specificity in an open and honest manner.

What Really Counts

Rearing a child who is gifted and talented is no easy task; negotiating school system bureaucracies on behalf of gifted children is not easy either. Parents thrust into this role by virtue of their child's needs must be consistent, open-minded, alert for alternatives, willing to act, and able to offer their child unwavering, unconditional love. However, even the most successful parents of gifted children come to points where they need others. An excellent way to "keep the faith" and to reinforce parents' active involvement in their child's education is to join with other parents who are in a similar position. Most school systems and states have gifted education advocacy groups that typically afford parents an opportunity to obtain information about gifted education. More importantly, such groups also offer parents a forum in which to interact with each other, keeping in mind that there is, in fact, strength in numbers. It is often helpful to know that you are not alone in your frustration with your child's collecting old shoe laces or that others have argued successfully for appropriate classroom placements. Further, parent associations can work wonders for maintaining your own logic and sense of humor, both of which are crucial for sending strong positive messages that you care and that you will not quit caring to the school and, most importantly, to your child.

VI. Resources

In order to assist parents in acquiring the information useful in fulfilling the roles needed for securing appropriate school services for gifted and talented children, a selected list of resources is provided. Reading materials are listed first and have been grouped according to topic. A listing of associations and other resources follows the reading suggestions.

A Selected List of Additional Readings

Affective/Social and Emotional Development

Buescher, T.M. (1987). Counseling gifted adolescents: A curriculum model for students, parents, and professionals. *Gifted Child Quarterly, 31,* 90–94.

Delisle, J.R. (1987). *Gifted kids speak out.* Minneapolis: Free Spirit.

Delisle, J.R. (1992). *Guiding the social and emotional development of gifted youth.* New York: Longman.

Olenchak, F.R. (1991). Wearing their shoes: Role playing to reverse underachievement. *Understanding Our Gifted, 3*(4), 1, 8–11.

Olenchak, F.R. (1994). Talent development: Accommodating the social and emotional needs of secondary gifted/learning disabled students. *Journal of Secondary Gifted Education, 5*(3), 40–52.

Silverman, L. (1983). Issues in affective development of the gifted. In J. VanTassel-Baska (Ed.), *A practical guide to counseling the gifted in a school setting* (pp. 6–21). Reston, VA: Council for Exceptional Children.

Silverman, L. (Ed.) (1993). *Counseling the gifted and talented.* Denver: Love.

Webb, J.T., Meckstroth, E.A., & Tolan, S.S. (1982). *Guiding the gifted child.* Columbus, OH: Ohio Psychology.

Zaffran, R.T., & Colangelo, N. (1979). *New voices in counseling the gifted.* Dubuque, IA: Kendall-Hunt.

Identification of the Gifted and Talented

Borland, J.H. (1986). IQ tests: Throwing out the bathwater, saving the baby. *Roeper Review, 8*(3), 163–167.

Feldhusen, J.F., Asher, J.W., & Hoover, S.M. (1984). Problems in the identification of giftedness, talent, or ability. *Gifted Child Quarterly, 28,* 149–156.

Ramos-Ford, V., & Gardner, H. (1991). Giftedness from a multiple intelligences perspective. In N. Colangelo & G. Davis (Eds.), *Handbook of gifted education.* Boston: Allyn and Bacon.

Renzulli, J.S. (1982). Dear Mr. and Mrs. Copernicus: We regret to inform you. *Gifted Child Quarterly, 26,* 11–14.

Sternberg, R.J. (1982). Lies we live by: Misapplication of tests in identifying the gifted. *Gifted Child Quarterly, 26,* 157–161.

Sternberg, R.J., & Davidson, J. (Eds.). (1986). *Conceptions of giftedness.* New York: Cambridge University Press.

Terman, L. (1925). *Genetic studies of genius* (Vol. 1). Stanford, CA: Stanford University Press.

Van Tassel-Baska, J. (1983). Profiles of precocity: The 1982 Midwest talent search finalists. *Gifted Child Quarterly, 27*(3), 139–144.

Weinberg, R. (1989). Intelligence and IQ: Landmark issues and great debates. *American Psychologist, 44*(2), 98–104.

Witty, P. (1930). *A study of one hundred gifted children.* Lawrence, KS: Bureau of School Service and Research.

Parent-Child-School Relationships

Colangelo, N., & Kelly, K.R. (1983). A study of student, parent, and teacher attitudes toward gifted programs and gifted students. *Gifted Child Quarterly, 27*, 107–110.

Comer, J.P. (1990). Home, school, and academic learning. In J.I. Goodlad & P. Keating (Eds.), *Access to knowledge: An agenda for our nation's schools.* New York: College Entrance Examination Board.

Goertzel, V., & Goertzel, M.G. (1962). *Cradles of eminence.* Boston: Little, Brown and Company.

Krueger, M.L. (1978). *On being gifted.* New York: Walker and Company.

Montemayer, R. (1984). Changes in parent and peer relationships between childhood and adolescence: A research agenda for gifted adolescents. *Journal for the Education of the Gifted, 8*(l), 9–23.

Purcell, J.H. (1993). The effects of the elimination of gifted and talented programs on participating students and their parents. *Gifted Child Quarterly, 37*(4), 177–187.

Sebring, A.D. (1983). Parental factors on the social and emotional adjustment of the gifted. *Roeper Review, 6*(2), 97–99.

Treffinger, D., & Fine, M. (1979). When there's a problem in school: Some guidelines for parents and teachers of gifted children. *G/C/T, 10*, 32–34.

Programs and Curriculum

Benbow, C.P. (1986). SYMPY's model for teaching mathematically precocious students. In J.S. Renzulli (Ed.), *Systems and models for developing programs for the gifted and talented.* Mansfield Center, CT: Creative Learning Press.

Feldhusen, J.F., & Kolloff, P.B. (1986). The Purdue three-stage enrichment model for gifted education at the elementary level. In J.S. Renzulli (Ed.), *Systems and models for developing programs for the gifted and talented.* Mansfield Center, CT: Creative Learning Press.

Feldhusen, J.F., & Robinson, A.W. (1986). The Purdue secondary model for gifted and talented youth. In J.S. Renzulli (Ed.), *Systems and models for developing programs for the gifted and talented.* Mansfield Center, CT: Creative Learning Press.

Feldhusen, J.F., & Treffinger, D.J. (1985). *Creative thinking and problem solving in gifted education* (3rd ed.). Dubuque, IA: Kendall-Hunt.

Genshaft, J.L., Bireley, M., & Hollinger, C.L. (Eds.). (1995). *Serving gifted and talented students: A resource for school personnel.* Austin, TX: Pro-Ed.

Maker, C.J., & Nielson, A.B. (1995). *Teaching models in education of the gifted.* Austin, TX: Pro-Ed.

Reis, S.M., & Renzulli, J.S. (1986). The secondary triad model. In J.S. Renzulli (Ed.), *Systems and models for developing programs for the gifted and talented.* Mansfield Center, CT: Creative Learning Press.

Renzulli, J.S. (1994). *Schools for talent development: A practical plan for total school improvement.* Mansfield Center, CT: Creative Learning Press.

Renzulli, J.S. (Ed.). (1986). *Systems and models for developing programs for the gifted and talented.* Mansfield Center, CT: Creative Learning Press.

Renzulli, J.S., & Reis, S.M. (1985). *The schoolwide enrichment model: A comprehensive plan for educational excellence.* Mansfield Center, CT: Creative Learning Press.

Renzulli, J.S., & Reis, S.M. (1986). The enrichment triad/revolving door model: A schoolwide plan for the development of creative productivity. In J.S. Renzulli (Ed.), *Systems and models for developing programs for the gifted and talented.* Mansfield Center, CT: Creative Learning Press.

Van Tassel-Baska, J. (1994). *Comprehensive curriculum for gifted learners.* Boston: Allyn and Bacon.

Special Areas of Giftedness: Gifted Girls

Benbow, C., & Stanley, J.C. (1980). Sex differences in mathematical ability: Fact or artifact? *Science, 210,* 1262–1264.

Callahan, C.M. (1979). The gifted and talented woman. In A.H. Passow (Ed.), *The gifted and the talented.* Chicago: National Society for the Study of Education.

Hollinger, C., & Fleming, E. (1988). Gifted and talented young women: Antecedents and correlates of life satisfaction. *Gifted Child Quarterly, 32,* 254–259.

Hollinger, C., & Fleming, E. (1992). A longitudinal examination of life choices of gifted and talented young women. *Gifted Child Quarterly, 36*(4), 207–212.

Kerr, B.A. (1985). *Smart girls, gifted women.* Columbus, OH: Psychology Publishing.

Kerr, B.A. (1991). Educating gifted girls. In N. Colangelo & G. Davis (Eds.), *Handbook of gifted education.* Boston: Allyn and Bacon.

Reis, S.M. (1987). We can't change what we don't recognize: Understanding the special needs of gifted females. *Gifted Child Quarterly, 31,* 83–89.

Reis, S.M., & Callahan, C.M. (1989). Gifted females: They've come a long way—or have they? *Journal for the Education of the Gifted, 12*(2), 99–117.

Reis, S.M., & Dobyns, S.M. (1991). An annotated bibliography of nonfictional books and curricular materials to encourage gifted females. *Roeper Review, 13*(3), 129–134.

Silverman, L.K. (1986). What happens in the gifted girl? In C.J. Maker (Ed.), *Critical issues in gifted education.* Rockville, MD: Aspen.

Silverman, L.K. (1991). Helping gifted girls reach their potential. *Roeper Review, 13*(3), 122–123.

Walker, B.A., Reis, S.M., & Leonard, J.S. (1992). A developmental investigation of the lives of gifted women. *Gifted Child Quarterly, 36*(4), 201–206.

Special Areas of Giftedness: Gifted with Cultural Diversity

Baldwin, A. (1987). Undiscovered diamonds. *Journal for the Education of the Gifted, 10*(4), 271–286.

Borland, J.H., & Wright, L. (1994). Identifying young, potentially gifted, economically disadvantaged students. *Gifted Child Quarterly, 38*(4), 164–171.

Frasier, M. (1991). Response to Kitano: The sharing of giftedness between culturally diverse and non-diverse students. *Journal for the Education of the Gifted, 15*(1), 20–30.

Ford, D.Y. (1993). Support for the achievement ideology and determinants of underachievement as perceived by gifted, above-average, and average Black students. *Journal for the Education of the Gifted, 16*(3), 28–298.

Kitano, M. (1991). A multicultural educational perspective on serving the culturally diverse gifted. *Journal for the Education of the Gifted, 15*(1), 4–19.

Maker, C.J. (1983). Quality education for gifted minority students. *Journal for the Education of the Gifted, 6*, 140–153.

Special Areas of Giftedness: Gifted with Disabilities

Baum, S. (1984). Meeting the needs of learning disabled gifted students. *Roeper Review, 7*, 16–19.

Baum, S., Owen, S.V., & Dixon, J. (1991). *To be gifted and learning disabled: From identification to practical intervention strategies.* Mansfield Center, CT: Creative Learning.

Coleman, M.R. (Ed.) (1994). *Journal of Secondary Gifted Education, 5*(3).

Fox, L., Brody, L., & Tobin, D. (Eds.). (1983). *Learning disabled/gifted children: Identification and programming.* Baltimore: University Park Press.

Karnes, M.B. (1979). Young handicapped children can be gifted and talented. *Journal for the Education of the Gifted, 2,* 157–172.

Karnes, M.B., Shwedel, A.M., & Lewis, G.F. (1983). Long-term effects of early programming for the gifted/talented handicapped. *Journal for the Education of the Gifted, 6,* 266–276.

Olenchak, F.R. (1995). Effects of enrichment on gifted/learning disabled students. *Journal for the Education of the Gifted, 18*(4), 385–399.

Whitmore, J.R., & Maker, J. (1985). *Intellectual giftedness in disabled persons.* Rockville, MD: Aspen.

Special Areas of Giftedness: Underachieving Gifted

Emerick, L.J. (1989). Student interests: A key to reversing the underachievement pattern. *Understanding Our Gifted, 2*(l), 1, 10–12.

Kaufmann, F. (1986). *Helping the muskrat guard his musk: A new look at underachievement.* Bossier City, LA: Bossier Parish Schools.

Lajoie, S.P., & Shore, B.M. (1981). Three myths? The over-representation of the gifted among dropouts, delinquents, and suicides. *Gifted Child Quarterly, 25,* 138–141.

Rimm, S.B. (1986). *Underachievement syndrome: Causes and cures.* Watertown, WI: Apple.

Rimm, S.B. (1991). Underachievement and superachievement: Flip sides of the same psychological coin. In N. Colangelo & G. Davis (Eds.), *Handbook of gifted education.* Boston: Allyn and Bacon.

Rimm, S.B., & Lowe, B. (1988). Family environments of underachieving gifted students. *Gifted Child Quarterly, 32,* 353–361.

Rimm, S.B., & Olenchak, F.R. (1991). How Future Problem Solving helps underachieving gifted students. *Gifted Child Today, 14*(2), 19–22.

Whitmore, J.R. (1980). *Giftedness, conflict, and underachievement.* Boston: Allyn and Bacon.

Whitmore, J.R. (1986). Understanding a lack of motivation to excel. *Gifted Child Quarterly, 30*(2), 66–69.

Whitmore, J.R. (1989). Reexamining the concept of underachievement. *Understanding Our Gifted, 2*(l), 1, 7–9.

Texts to Enhance Parenting

Alvino, J., & *Gifted Children Newsletter* Staff (1985). *Parents guide to raising a gifted child: Recognizing and development of your child's potential.* New York: Little, Brown.

Alvino, J., & *Gifted Children Monthly* Editors (1989). *Parents' guide to raising a gifted toddler: Recognizing and developing the potential of your child from birth to five years.* New York: Little, Brown.

Delisle, J.R. (1984). *Gifted children speak out.* New York: Walker.

Engel, J. (1988). *It's o.k. to be gifted or talented.* New York: Tor.

Gladieux, R. (1988). *How to parent gifted children: A mother's experiences and insights.* Manassas, VA: Gifted Education Press.

Karnes, F.A., & Marquardt, R.G. (1991). *Gifted children and legal issues in education: Parents' stories of hope.* Dayton, OH: Ohio Psychology Press.

Mallis, J. (1992). *Diamonds in the dust: Discover and develop your child's gifts* (2nd ed.). Austin, TX: Multi Media Arts.

Miller, A. (1994). *The drama of the gifted child: The search for true self.* New York: Basic.

Riley, J., & Carlson, M. (1984). *Help for parents of gifted and talented children.* Carthage, IL: Good Apple.

Rimm, S.B. (1994). *Keys to parenting the gifted child.* Hauppauge, NY: Barron.

Smutny, J.F. (1991). *Your gifted child: How to recognize and develop the special talents in your child from birth to age seven.* New York: Ballentine.

Takacs, C.A. (1986). *Enjoy your gifted child.* Syracuse, NY: Syracuse University Press.

A Selected List of Associations and Other Resources for Parents

Associations for Parents and Educators

Association for the Education of Gifted Underachieving Students (AEGUS)
4414 S. Eagle Village Rd.
Manlius, NY 13104-9773
(205) 348-7340

The Association for the Gifted (TAG)
1920 Association Dr.
Reston, VA 22091
(800) 336-3278

National Association for Creative Children and Adults
8080 Spring Valley Dr.
Cincinnati, OH 45236
(513) 631-1777

National Association for Gifted Children (NAGC)
1707 L St., N.W., Suite 550
Washington, DC 20036
(202) 785-4268

Parent Information Network for the Gifted (PING)
190 Rock Rd.
Glen Rock, NJ 07542-1736
(900) 773-7464; (201) 444-6530

State-Level Gifted Education Contacts

Alaska
Dr. Richard Smiley
Program Manager
Gifted and Talented
Education
Alaska Office of Special
Services
Alaska Department of
Education
801 W. 10th St., Suite 200
Juneau, AK 99801-1894
(907) 465-8702
(907) 465-3396 (fax)

Alabama
Linda Grill
Education Specialist
Special Education Services
Alabama Department of
Education
Gordon Persons Bldg.
Box 302101
Montgomery, AL 36130-
2101
(334) 242-8114
lgrill@sdenet.alsde.edu

Arkansas
Ann Biggers
Administrator
Office of Gifted and
Talented
Arkansas Department of
Education
Education Bldg., Room 103-B
4 State Capitol Mall
Little Rock, AR 72201
(501) 682-4224
abiggers@arkedu.k12.ar.us

Arizona
Dr. Nancy Stahl
Gifted Program Specialist
Arizona Department of
Education
1535 W. Jefferson
Phoenix, AZ 85007
(602) 542-7836

California
Kathy Marshall
Consultant
Gifted & Talented Education

California Department of
Education
P.O. Box 944272
Sacramento, CA 94244-2720
(916) 657-5257
(916) 657-5112 (fax)

California
Ruth Wharton
Consultant
Gifted and Talented Education
California Department of
Education
P.O. Box 944272
Sacramento, CA 94244-2720
(916) 657-5257
(916) 657-5112 (fax)

Colorado
Frank Rainey
Consultant
Gifted and Talented
Education
Colorado Department of
Education
201 E. Colfax, Rm. 402
Denver, CO 80203
(303) 866-6849
(303) 830-0793 (fax)
rainey_f@cde.state.co.us

Connecticut
(vacant)
Consultant
Gifted and Talented Programs

Connecticut Department of
Education
25 Industrial Park Rd.
Middletown, CT 06457
(203) 638-4247

District of Columbia
(no position)
Gifted / Talented Education
D.C. Public Schools
Rabaut Administration Bldg.
N. Dakota & Kansas
avenues., N.W.
Washington, DC 20011
(202) 576-6171

Delaware
Dr. Margaret S. Dee
Education Associate
Gifted and Talented Program
Delaware Department of
Public Instruction
P.O. Box 1402
Townsend Building
Dover, DE 19903
(302) 739-4667
(302) 739-2388 (fax)

Florida
Shirley Perkins
Program Specialist
Bureau of Student Services
and Exceptional Education
Florida Department of
Education

Florida Education Center,
Suite 614
Tallahassee, FL 32399-0400
(850) 488-1106
(850) 922-7088 (fax)

Georgia
Sally Krisel
Specialist
Gifted Education/
Curriculum Services
Georgia Department of
Education
1770 Twin Towers East
Atlanta, GA 30334-5040
(404) 657-0182
(404) 657-7096 (fax)

Guam
Teri Knapp
GATE Coordinator
Gifted and Talented Education
Guam Department of
Education
P.O. Box DE
Agana, GU 96910
(671) 475-0598

Hawaii
Betsy Moneymaker
Early Childhood / Gifted
Education Specialist
Student Support Services
Hawaii Department of
Education

637 18th Ave., Bldg. C, #204
Honolulu, HI 96816
(808) 733-4476
(808) 733-4475 (fax)

Idaho
Gary Marx
Gifted/Talented Specialist
Special Education Services
Idaho Department of
Education
P.O. Box 83720
Boise, ID 83720-0027
(208) 332-6920
(208) 334-4664 (fax)
gmarx@sde.state.id.us

Illinois
Susan Morrison
Education Consultant
Gifted and Talented Education
Illinois Board of Education
100 N. First St.
Springfield, IL 62777
(217) 782-3371

Indiana
Patti Garrett
Program Manager
Gifted and Talented Education
Indiana Department of
Education
State House, Room 229
Indianapolis, IN 46204-2798
(317) 232-9106

Iowa
Dr. Maryellen Knowles
Consultant
Gifted and Talented
Education
Iowa Department of
Education
Grimes State Office Building
Des Moines, IA 50319-0146
(515) 281-3199
mknowle@max.state.ia.us

Kansas
Joan R. Miller
Program Consultant
Gifted and Talented Education
Kansas State Board of
Education
Special Education
Administration
120 S.E. 10th Ave.
Topeka, KS 66612-1182
(785) 296-3857
(785) 296-7933 (fax)
jmiller@smtpgw.kabe.
state.ks.us

Kentucky
Dr. Laura Pehkonen
Consultant
Gifted and Talented Education
Kentucky Department of
Education
Division of Professional
Development

500 Mero St., 17th Floor
Frankfort, KY 40601
(502) 564-2672
(502) 564-6952 (fax)
lpehkone@kde.state.ky.us

Louisiana
Eileen Kendrick
Coordinator
Gifted and Talented Program
Louisiana Department of
Education
P.O. Box 94064
Baton Rouge, LA 70804-
9064
(504) 763-3942
(504) 763-3937 (fax)
ekendrick@mail.doc.
state.la.us

Maine
Valerie Terry Seaberg
Consultant
Gifted and Talented Education
Maine Department of
Education
State House Station #23
Augusta, ME 04333
(207) 287-5950
(207) 287-5900 (fax)

Maryland
Dr. Carolyn R. Cooper
Section Chief
Student Achievement/Gifted

and Talented Education
Maryland Department of
Education
200 W. Baltimore St.
Baltimore, MD 21201-2595
(410) 767-0363
(410) 333-2379 (fax)

Massachusetts
Deborah Smith-Pressley
Instructional & Curriculum
Services
Massachusetts Department
of Education
350 Main St.
Malden, MA 02148
(617) 388-3300, ext. 260
(617) 388-3395 (fax)

Michigan
Mary Bailey-Hengesh
Consultant for Talent
Development
Curriculum Development
Program
Michigan Department of
Education
P.O. Box 30008
Lansing, MI 48909
(517) 373-4213

Minnesota
Mary S. Pfeifer
Office of Teaching & Learning
Children, Families, and

Learning Department
624 Capitol Square
550 Cedar St.
St. Paul, MN 55101
(612) 297-7204

Mississippi
Dr. Conrad S. Castle
Consultant
Gifted and Talented Programs
Mississippi Department of
Education, Rm.. 372
Office of Deputy
Superintendent
P.O. Box 771
Jackson, MS 39205-0771
(601) 359-3588
(601) 359-2326 (fax)

Missouri
David Welch
Director
Gifted Education Programs
Missouri Department of
Elem & Secondary Education
P.O. Box 480
Jefferson City, MO 65102
(573) 751-2453
(573) 751-9434 (fax)
dwelch@mail.dese.state.mo.us

Montana
Michael Hall
Contact
Gifted Education and

Instructional Technology
Montana Office of Public
Instruction
P.O. Box 202501
Helena, MT 59620-2501
(406) 444-4422
(406) 444-1373 (fax)
mhall@opi.mt.gov

North Carolina
Rebecca B. Garland
Consultant
Gifted Education Programs
North Carolina Department
of Public Instruction
Exceptional Children
Division
301 N. Wilmington St.
Raleigh, NC 27601-2825
(919) 715-1999

North Dakota
Ann Clapper
Director
Curriculum Leadership &
Improvement
North Dakota Department
of Public Instruction
State Univ. Station Box 5036
Fargo, ND 58105-5036
(701) 231-6030

Nebraska
Janis McKenzie
Director

High-Ability Learner Education
Nebraska Department of
Education
301 Centennial Mall South,
Box 94987
Lincoln, NE 68509-4987
(402) 471-0737 (M/T); 463-
5611 (W–F); (402) 471-
0117 (fax, M/T); 463-9555
(fax, W–F)
Janis_m@nde4.nde.state.ne.us

New Hampshire
Michele Munson
Consultant
Office of Gifted Education
New Hampshire
Department of Education
101 Pleasant St.
Concord, NH 03301
(603) 271-3769

New Jersey
Roberta Carol
Coordinator
Gifted and Talented Education
New Jersey Department of
Education
100 Riverview, CN 500
Trenton, NJ 08625
(609) 984-1805

New Mexico
Dr. Wayne Gordon
Consultant

Special Education
Department
New Mexico Department of
Education
435 St. Michael's Drive
Building D
Santa Fe, NM 87505
(505) 827-6541
(505) 827-6791 (fax)

Nevada
Doris B. Betts
Gifted and Talented Education
Nevada Department of
Education
700 E. Fifth St., Capitol
Complex
Carson City, NV 89701
(702) 687-9141
(702) 687-5660 (fax)

New York
Mary Daley
Executive Director
New York State Summer
Institutes
New York State Education
Department
Room 981 EBA
Albany, NY 12234
(518) 474-8773

Ohio
Janet Schultz
Gifted Education Consultant

Division of Special Education
Ohio Department of Education
933 High St.
Worthington, OH 43085-
4087
(614) 466-2650
(614) 752-1429 (fax)
se_schultz@ode.ohio.gov

Oklahoma
Anita Boone
Coordinator
Gifted and Talented Section
Oklahoma Department of
Education
2500 N. Lincoln Blvd.
Oklahoma City, OK 73105-
4599
(918) 333-2079
aboone@aol.com

Oklahoma
Kristy Ehlers
Director
Gifted and Talented
Education Division
Oklahoma Department of
Education
2500 N. Lincoln Blvd.
Oklahoma City, OK 73105-
4599
(405) 521-4287
(405) 521-2971 (fax)
Kristy_Ehlers@mail.sde.state.
ok.us

Oregon
Nancy Anderson
Education Specialist
Gifted and Talented
Programs
Oregon Department of
Education
255 Capitol St., N.E.
Salem, OR 97310-0290
(503) 378-3598

Pennsylvania
T. Noretta Bingaman
Director
Gifted Technical Assistance
Program
Pennsylvania Department of
Education
Bureau of Special Education,
7th Floor
333 Market St.
Harrisburg, PA 17126-0333
(717) 783-6913

Puerto Rico
Ivonne Quinonez
Gifted and Talented Education
Puerto Rico Department of
Education
P.O. Box 190759
San Juan, PR 00919-0759
(809) 274-1059

Rhode Island
Ina S. Woolman

Coordinator
Gifted and Talented
Programs
Rhode Island Department of
Elementary & Secondary
Education
255 Westminister St., Rm. 400
Providence, RI 02903-3400
(401) 277-4600, ext. 2318
(401) 277-6030 (fax)
iwoolman@worldnet.att.net

South Carolina
Cindy Saylor
Gifted and Talented
Education Contact
South Carolina Department
of Education
803-A Rutledge Bldg.
1429 Senate St.
Columbia, SC 29201
(803) 734-8371
(803) 734-6142 (fax)

South Dakota
Shirlie Hoag
Gifted Education
South Dakota Department
of Education
700 Governors Drive
Pierre, SD 57501-2291
(605) 773-6400

Tennessee
Ann Sanders

Coordinator
Gifted and Talented
Programs and Services
Tennessee Department of
Education
Division of Special Education
710 James Robertson Pkwy.,
8th Floor
Nashville, TN 37243-0380
(615) 741-7811
(615) 532-9412 (fax)
asanders@mail.state.tn.us

Texas
Evelyn L. Hiatt
Director
Gifted and Talented Education
Texas Education Agency
1701 N. Congress Ave.
Austin, TX 78701
(512) 463-9455
(512) 305-8920 (fax)

Utah
Connie Love
Specialist
Gifted and Talented Education
Utah Office of Education
250 E. 500 South
Salt Lake City, UT 84111
(801) 538-7743
(801) 538-7769 (fax)

Virginia
Joy L. Baytops

Specialist
Programs for the Gifted
Virginia Department of
Education
Office of Elementary and
Middle School
P.O. Box 2120
Richmond, VA 23218-2120
(804) 371-7419
(804) 786-1703 (fax)

St. Thomas/St. John
Mary Harley
Coordinator
Gifted and Talented Education
St. Thomas/St. John School
District
#44-46 Kongens Gade
St. Thomas, VI 00802
(809) 775-2250

Vermont
(no position designated)
Gifted and Talented Education
Vermont Department of
Education
120 State St.
Montpelier, VT 05620
(802) 828-3111

Washington
Gayle Pauley
Program Supervisor
Gifted and Talented Education
Washington Office of Public

Instruction
Instructional Programs
Old Capitol Bldg., Box 47200
Olympia, WA 98504-7200
(360) 753-2858
(360) 586-2728 (fax)
gpauley@inspire.ospi.
wednet.edu

Wisconsin
(no position)
Gifted and Talented
Education
Wisconsin Department of
Public Instruction
125 S. Webster St.
P.O. Box 7841
Madison, WI 53707
(608) 266-3560

West Virginia
Dr. Virginia Simmons

Coordinator of Gifted
Programs
Office of Special Education
West Virginia Department of
Education
Capitol Complex
Building 6, Room 362
Charleston, WV 25305
(304) 558-0160
vsimmons@access.k12.wv.us

Wyoming
Kathy Scheurman
Gifted and Talented
Education
Wyoming Department of
Education
Hathaway Building, 2nd
Floor
2300 Capitol Avenue
Cheyenne, WY 82002
(307) 777-7843

Journals and Magazines for Parents and Educators

Advanced Development
Institute for the Study of Advanced Development
777 Pearl St.
Denver, CO 80302

Creative Child and Adult Quarterly
8080 Spring Valley Dr.
Cincinnati, OH 45236
(513) 631-1777

Gifted Child Quarterly
1707 L St. N.W., Suite 550
Washington, DC 20036
(202) 785-4268

Gifted Child Today
P.O. Box 8813
Waco, TX 76714-8813
(800) 998-2208
(800) 240-0333 (fax)

Gifted Education Review
P.O. Box 2278
Evergreen, CO 80439-2278

Journal for the Education of the Gifted
The University of North Carolina Press
P.O. Box 2288
Chapel Hill, NC 27515-2288
(919) 966-3561

Journal of Creative Behavior
Creative Educational Foundation
1050 Union Road
Buffalo, NY 14224

Journal of Secondary Gifted Education
P.O. Box 8813
Waco, TX 76714-8813
(800) 998-2208
(800) 240-0333 (fax)

Parenting for High Potential
1707 L St. N.W., Suite 550
Washington, DC 20036

Roeper Review
P.O. Box 329
Bloomfield Hills, MI 48303-0329
(810) 642-1500

Understanding Our Gifted
Open Space Communications
P.O. Box 18268
Boulder, CO 80308-8268
(303) 444-7020

Magazines and Books for School-Aged Youth

Children's books in print: 1995. (1994). Author Index, Title Index, Illustrator Index. New Providence, NJ: R.R. Bowker.
Hauser, P., & Nelson, G.A. (1988). *Books for the gifted child.* New Providence, NJ: R.R. Bowker.
Katz, B. (1987). *Magazines for school libraries.* New Providence, NJ: R.R. Bowker.
Stoll, D.P. (Ed.) (1994). *Magazines for kids and teens.* Glassboro, NJ: Educational Press Association of America.

Programs and Contests
for Children Involving Parent Assistance

Freed, J.M. (1994). *Freed's guide to student contests and publishing* (5th ed.). Delaware, OH: Fountainpen Press.
Long, K. (1991). *Directory of educational contests for students K–12.* Santa Barbara, CA: ABC-Clio.
National Committee on Contests and Activities (1994). *NASSP national advisory list of contests and activities.* Reston, VA: National Association of Secondary School Principals.
Snodgrass, M.E. (Ed.) (1991). *Comntests for students: All you need to know to enter and win 600 contests.* Detroit: Gale Research.

VII. Glossary of Terms

acceleration: Skills and/or content are addressed at a pace and a level of difficulty that are advanced from the norm. If accomplished by grade level, children are "skipped" over grades; a child who leaps from grade three to grade five without having been in fourth grade is an example. If accomplished by content, children complete subject material at an age earlier than the norm and/or at a pace that is quicker than usual; a child who completes biology one year early or one who condenses a year of English into one quarter are examples.

affective needs: Gifted and talented students, by virtue of their particular abilities and potential, tend to have specific social and emotional needs that must be addressed by both school and home. For example, because gifted and talented youngsters generally have higher levels of internal control and responsibility, they often set high goals for themselves that may be difficult to achieve. When such goals are not readily met, natural outcomes of frustration, disappointment, and feelings of ineptitude must be handled.

curriculum compacting: Individuals or groups of students are assessed for level of academic performance in order to reduce or eliminate required lessons and assignments that are either repetitious or can be mastered in less time than is normally required. By streamlining the basic curriculum, students are less likely to be bored by unchallenging or previously-mastered basic skills work, and time can be freed from the regular school day for pursuit of accelerated and/or enriched work.

enrichment: Experiences and activities are scheduled that are above and beyond the basic curriculum offered in the classroom or the school. While pace is considered, the level of difficulty is more important in that children are presented opportunities to expand beyond the basic material. The emphasis is on breadth of knowledge as opposed to worrying about speed or level.

gifted and talented: Although sometimes these terms are used separately, together they generally are intended to signify persons who are highly capable in terms of general intellectual ability, specific academic aptitude, creative/productive thinking, leadership ability, and visual and performing arts. These individuals require specialized types of educational programs in order to develop their potential adequately for self and society. Some professionals believe giftedness and talent can be identified *a priori* (in advance of actual demonstrated productivity). Others feel that only *potential* for such productive behavior can be identified in an *a priori* manner and that, ultimately, giftedness and talent must be demonstrated in order to be absolutely identified. Today, few professionals define giftedness and talent in terms of a single test score.

heterogeneous groups: Students are grouped into classes at random without particular regard for abilities. While a number of homogenous groupings take place in heterogeneous classrooms, these groups tend to be fluid and flexible in nature and should not be confused with permanent ability tracks. Advocates defend this grouping method because it is said to represent more closely the diversity of abilities present in the workaday world. Critics feel this approach, if used exclusively, denies gifted and talented students adequate time together to stimulate each other. In most locales, learning environments called "regular classrooms" are most usually of this type.

homogeneous groups: Classes are arranged so that students enrolled in each one represent nearly the same types of abilities. Sometimes called "ability grouping," this is a method for teaching groups of students for whom, based on their similar abilities, it is assumed educational needs are the same. As noted above, heterogenous classes often include homogenous groups as a means for teaching groups of students with similar abilities and needs. Examples of homogeneous classes are accelerated and honors groups. Advocates defend this grouping method based on research supporting its benefits for gifted and talented students at least for some of the time spent in school. Critics view the approach as elitist when such groupings become permanent as opposed to fluid and temporary for particular needs as they arise.

identification of gifted and talented students: A process used by professionals that encompasses many sources of information about a child. These may include data from tests, parent surveys, teacher referrals, interviews with the child, observations, peer nominations, and any other sources from which professionals might be able to form as thorough a picture of the child's abilities as possible. Usually, these data are reviewed by a screening or identification committee composed of school district and community representatives who compare the information gathered about a child against some preestablished set of criteria for identification. Criteria can be set at the local, district, or state levels in the absence of specific federal requirements.

individualized education program (IEP): Developed as a component of federal legislation on behalf of children who have disabilities, some gifted and talented programs on either a state or local level have adopted this process. A team of professionals, working jointly with parents, creates a specific set of goals and objectives that are personally tailored to the educational needs of each individual child. Instead of the child being expected to adapt to all that school presents, the school program is adjusted according to the individual child's educational needs as measured by tests and other data.

precocious: Occasionally, this term is used interchangeably with "gifted and talented," though it is generally used to indicate children who have demonstrated certain kinds of aptitudes earlier in life than would be expected of most children of the same age.

VIII. References

Anyon, J. (1987). Social class and the hidden curriculum of work. In E. Stevens & G.H. Woods (Eds.), *Justice, ideology, and education: An introduction to the social foundations of education* (pp. 210–226). New York: Random House.

Benbow, C.P. (1986). SMPY's model for teaching mathematically precocious students. In J.S. Renzulli (Ed.), *Systems and models for developing programs for the gifted and talented.* Mansfield Center, CT: Creative Learning Press.

Benbow, C.P., & Stanley, J.C. (1982). Intellectually talented boys and girls: Educational profiles. *Gifted Child Quarterly, 26*(2), 82–88.

Benbow, C.P., & Stanley, J.C. (1983). *Academic precocity: Aspects of its development.* Baltimore: Johns Hopkins University Press.

Bernstein, H.T. (1985). The new politics of textbook adoption. *Phi Delta Kappan, 66,* 463–466.

Bloom, B.S. (1982). The role of gifts and markers in the development of talent. *Exceptional Children, 48*(6), 510–522.

Bloom, B.S. (1985). *Developing talent in young people.* New York: Ballentine Books.

Chall, J.S., & Conrad, S.S. (1991). *Should textbooks challenge students? The case for easier or harder textbooks.* New York: Teachers College Press.

Clark, B. (1988). *Growing up gifted* (3rd ed.). Columbus, OH: Merrill.

Council of State Directors of Programs for the Gifted (1985). *The state of the states' gifted and talented education.* Augusta, ME: Maine Department of Education.

Cuban, L. (1982). Persistence of the inevitable: The teacher-centered classroom. *Education and Urban Society, 15*(1), 26–41.

Delisle, J.R. (1992). *Guiding the social and emotional development of gifted youth.* New York: Longman.

Educational Products Information Exchange Institute (1981). *Educational Research and Development Report, 3*(4).

Federal Register (1992, March 13). Education of the gifted and talented. Washington, DC: U.S. Government Printing Office, 8997.

Feldman, D.H. (1988). Creativity: Dreams, insights, and transformations. In R.J. Sternberg (Ed.), *The nature of creativity.* New York: Cambridge University Press.

Flavell, J.H. (1985). *Cognitive development.* Englewood Cliffs, NJ: Prentice-Hall.

Gallagher, J. (1985). *Teaching the gifted child* (3rd ed.). Boston: Allyn and Bacon.

Gallagher, J., & Gallagher, S. (1994). *Teaching the gifted child* (4th ed.). Boston: Allyn and Bacon.

Gardner, H. (1983). *Frames of mind: The theory of multiple intelligences.* New York: Basic Books.

Gardner, H. (1985). *The mind's new science: A history of the cognitive revolution.* New York: Basic Books.

Gardner, H. (1993). *Multiple intelligences: The theory in practice.* New York: Basic Books.

Goertzel, V., & Goertzel, M.G. (1962). *Cradles of eminence.* Boston: Little, Brown.

Goodlad, J.I. (1983). A study of schooling; Some findings and hypotheses. *Phi Delta Kappan, 64*(2), 113–118.

Jackson, R.M., Cleveland, J.C., & Mirenda, P.F. (1975). The longitudinal effects of early identification and counseling of underachievers. *Journal of School Psychology, 13,* 119–128.

Keating, D.P. (Ed.). (1976). *Intellectual talent: Research and development.* Baltimore: Johns Hopkins University Press.

Kirst, M.W. (1982). How to improve schools without spending more money. *Phi Delta Kappan, 64*(l), 6–8.

Kulik, J.A., & Kulik, C.C. (1991). Research on acceleration. In N. Colangelo & G.A. Davis (Eds.). *Handbook of gifted education.* Boston: Allyn and Bacon.

Marland, S.P. (1972). *Education of the gifted and talented: Report to the Congress of the United States by the U.S. Commissioner of Education.* Washington: U.S. Government Printing Office.

Olenchak, F.R. (1988). The schoolwide enrichment model in elementary schools: A study of implementation stages and the effects on educational excellence. In J.S. Renzulli (Ed.), *Technical report of research studies related to the revolving door identification model* (2nd ed.). Storrs, CT: Bureau of Educational Research, The University of Connecticut.

Olenchak, F.R. (1990). School change through gifted education: Effects on elementary students' attitudes toward learning. *Journal for the Education of the Gifted, 14*(l), 66–78.

Olenchak, F.R. (1991). Wearing their shoes: Role playing to reverse underachievement. *Understanding Our Gifted, 3*(4), 1, 8–11.

Olenchak, F.R. (1994). Talent development: Accommodating the social and emotional needs of secondary gifted/learning disabled students. *Journal of Secondary Gifted Education, 5*(3), 40–52.

Olenchak, F.R., & Renzulli, J.S. (1989). The effectiveness of the schoolwide enrichment model on selected aspects of elementary school change. *Gifted Child Quarterly, 33,* 36–46.

Pendarvis, E.D., Howley, A.A., & Howley, C.B. (1990). *The abilities of gifted children.* Englewood Cliffs, NJ: Prentice Hall.

Reis, S.M., Burns, D.E., Renzulli, J.S. (1992). *Curriculum compacting: The complete guide to modifying the regular cur-*

riculum for high ability students. Mansfield Center, CT: Creative Learning Press.

Reis, S.M., Westberg, K.L., Kulikowich, J., Caillard, F., Hebert, T., Plucker, J., Purcell, J.H., Rogers, J.B., & Smist, J.M. (1993). *Why not let high ability students start school in January? The curriculum compacting study.* (Research Monograph No. 93106). Storrs, CT: The National Research Center on the Gifted and Talented.

Renzulli, J.S. (1977). *The enrichment triad model: A guide for developing defensible programs for the gifted and talented.* Mansfield Center, CT: Creative Learning Press.

Renzulli, J.S. (1978). What makes giftedness? Reexamining a definition. *Phi Delta Kappan, 60,* 180–184.

Renzulli, J.S. (1985). The three-ring conception of giftedness: A developmental model for creative productivity. In R. Sternberg & J. Davidson (Eds.), *Conceptions of giftedness.* New York: Cambridge University Press.

Renzulli, J.S. (1994). *Schools for talent development: A practical plan for total school improvement.* Mansfield Center, CT: Creative Learning Press.

Renzulli, J.S., & Reis, S.M. (1985). *The schoolwide enrichment model: A comprehensive plan for educational excellence.* Mansfield Center, CT: Creative Learning Press.

Renzulli, J.S., Smith, L.H., & Reis, S.M. (1982). Curriculum compacting: An essential strategy for working with gifted students. *Elementary School Journal, 82,* 185–194.

Schack, G.D. (1986). *Creative productivity and self-efficacy in children.* Unpublished doctoral dissertation, University of Connecticut.

Simonton, D.K. (1984). *Genius, creativity, and leadership.* Cambridge, MA: Harvard University Press.

Stanley, J.C. (1985). A baker's dozen of years applying all four aspects of the study of mathematically precocious youth (SMPY). *Roeper Review, 7*(3), 170–173.

Stanley, J.C., & Benbow, C.P. (1983). Educating mathematically precocious youths: Twelve policy recommendations. *Educational Researcher, 11*(5), 4–9.

Stanley, J.C., & Benbow, C.P. (1986). Extremely young college graduates: Evidence of their success. *College and University, 58,* 361–371.

Stanley, J.C., Keating, D.P., & Fox, L.H. (Eds.) (1974). *Mathematical talent: Discovery, description, and development.* Baltimore: Johns Hopkins University Press.

Starko, A.J. (1986). *The effects of creative production on extracurricular creativity.* Unpublished doctoral dissertation, University of Connecticut.

Sternberg, R.J. (1981). A componential theory of intellectual giftedness. *Gifted Child Quarterly, 25*(2), 86–93.

Sternberg, R.J. (1982). Lies we live by: Misapplication of tests in identifying the gifted. *Gifted Child Quarterly, 26*(4), 157–161.

Sternberg, R.J. (1985). *Intelligence applied.* New York: Harcourt, Brace, Jovanovich.

Sternberg, R.J. (1986). A triarchic theory of intellectual giftedness. In R.J. Sternberg & J.E. Davidson (Eds.), *Conceptions of giftedness.* New York: Cambridge University Press.

Sternberg, R.J. (1988). *The triarchic mind.* New York: Viking.

Swassing, R.H. (Ed.). (1985). *Teaching gifted children and adolescents.* Columbus, OH: Merrill.

Taylor, B.M., & Frye, B.J. (1988). Pretesting: Minimize time spent on skill work for intermediate readers. *The Reading Teacher, 42*(2), 100–103.

VanTassel-Baska, J. (1981). *An administrator's guide to the education of gifted and talented children.* Washington: National Association of State Boards of Education.

Wilcox, K. (1982). Differential socialization in the classroom: Implications for equal opportunity. In G. Spindler (Ed.), *Doing the ethnography of schooling.* New York: CBS College.

Table 1

Characteristics of Gifted and Talented Students

I. General Intellectual Ability	II. Specific Academic Ability	III. Creative Ability	IV. Leadership Ability	V. Visual and Performing Arts Ability	VI. Psychomotor Ability
A. Learning 1. Awareness: acute observational power 2. Curiosity: wide and varied range of interests 3. Observation: keen and detailed 4. Collecting: accumulates many and varied items 5. Abstraction: comprehends abstract ideas with minimal concrete experience 6. Knowledge: has storehouse of information on various topics 7. Memory: facility for recall of previously learned material without extensive rote drill	A. Reads at advanced level for age or grade B. Express self clearly, either orally or in writing or both C. Good coordination, especially in eye-hand situations related to academic area(s) of strength D. Spends time beyond assignments in areas of interest E. Not easily discouraged by failure in projects or experiments F. Spends time on special	A. Curious about many things; asks questions about almost everything B. Generates new and unique ideas and solutions to problems C. Uninhibited in expression of opinion; sometimes radical and tenacious in disagreement D. High risk taker; adventuresome and speculative E. Intellectually manipulative; fantasizes and manipulates ideas; likes to adapt, improve, and modify institutions,	A. Carries out responsibilities well B. Self-confident with peers and adults C. Seems well-liked by at least some peers D. Cooperative with peers and adults E. Good verbal self expression; readily understood by others F. Adapts readily to new situations; flexible in thought and action G. Sociable; willingly participates in social activities	A. Artistic 1. Likes to participate in art activities; eager to express ideas visually 2. Incorporates large number of elements into art; varies subject and content of art work 3. Arrives at novel, unconventional solutions to artistic problems; unwilling to accept conventional ways of doing things 4. Concentrates for long periods of time on art work 5. Willingly tries different media; experiments with a variety of techniques and materials 6. Tends to select art media for free time activity	A. Energetic; seems to need and enjoy considerable physical exercise B. Enjoys participating in highly competitive games C. Consistently outstanding in different kinds of games D. One of the fastest runners in the class E. One of the most coordinated in the class F. Likes sports; either individual or team types of sports or both

8. Verbosity: proficiency with vocabulary advanced for age level

9. Reading:
   a. above average ability for age
   b. self-directed, often preferring non-fiction and biographies

10. Reasoning: quick analytical power, recognizing relationships easily

11. Critical thinking: tends toward skepticism; evaluative thought

12. Originality: use of unusual methods or ideas to solve problems and to create new items, procedures, or approaches

13. Can become mired in own ideas to point of isolation

14. Tendency to share so much as if a "know it all"

projects of his/her own related to interests and specific subjects areas of strength

G. Likes literature and discussion about specific academic area(s) of strength and interest

H. Excels in assignments and projects related to one or more specific academic subject areas relating to self-selected interests

I. Narrow range of high ability can restrict development in other areas

J. Perfectionism in ability area can develop

objects, and systems

F. Sees humor in situations that others do not see

G. Free in expression; open to the irrational in self

H. Sensitive to aesthetics

I. Nonconforming; accepting of seeming disorder; not interested in details

J. Critical; unwilling to accept authoritarian pronouncements without critical analysis

K. Independent nature can lead to conflict with rules, systems, traditions

L. Taking risks can grow to dangerous levels

M. Unusual ideas may garner peer criticism lead-

in and out of school

H. Tends to dominate others but without being viewed as "bossy"

I. Excels in athletics; good coordination

J. Good at judging abilities of others and placing them in roles appropriate for completing a task

K. Often consulted by peers for ideas and suggestions

L. Enters activities with contagious enthusiasm

M. Leads in differing types of activities

N. Elected to offices

O. Identifies steps toward a goal and then organizes

7. Especially sensitive to the environment; keen observer, seeing the unusual that may be overlooked by others

8. Produces balance and order in art work

9. Critical of own work, setting high standards of quality; often reworks and refines creations

10. Interested in art work of others; spends time studying and discussing art

11. Elaborates on ideas of others; uses them as "jumping off point" as opposed to copying them

12. Can be stubborn about tastes in art

B. Dramatic

1. Volunteers to participate in plays or skits

2. Easily tells a story or gives an account

3. Effectively uses gestures, facial, and body expressions to communicate

G. Willingly practices physical activities to enhance performance

H. May resort to physical activities at inappropriate times

B. Motivation

1. Questioning: seeks answers to wide range of questions; inquisitive; questions purposes of activities; intellectually curious

2. Interests: current and political events; concern for societal problems

3. Energy: high level of enthusiasm and alertness for some activities

4. Concentration: intense; long attention for activities of self-selected interest

5. Persistence: becomes absorbed in a task or problem until completion

6. Speed and Accuracy: learns new knowledge, skills, and concepts quickly and accurately

7. Impatience:

ing to isolationism

things and others to accomplish them

P. Bossy behavior may develop if given too much authority

Q. Confidence can create inability to handle failure

4. Adept at role playing, improvising, acting out situations "on the spot"

5. Can readily identify self with moods and motivations of story characters

6. Handles body with ease and poise for age

7. Creates own plays or develops plays from stories

8. Commands and holds attention of group when speaking

9. Able to evoke emotional responses from listeners

10. Imitates others easily

11. May overrely on demonstrative behavior to make a point

C. Musical

1. Shows sustained interest in music; seeks opportunities to hear and create music

2. Perceives fine dif-

ferences in tone (pitch, volume, timbre, duration)

3. Easily recalls melodies can accurately reproduce them

4. Eagerly participates in musical activities

5. Plays a musical instrument or indicates a strong desire to do so

6. Sensitive to rhythm of music; responds through body movement to changes in tempo

7. Aware of and can identify a variety of sounds, able to distinguish among background, chords, accompaniment, melody

8. Can become absorbed in music to exclusion of others

D. Dance

1. Responds to musical rhythm with body movements

2. Coordination is good for age

disinterested in details, testy with those who learn or respond less rapidly

8. Perfectionism: self-critical and often dissatisfied with own efforts and products

9. Evaluative: concerned with moral issues, right and wrong, cause and effect; judgmental of people, events, things

10. Independence: likes self-direction

11. Conformity: individualistic; nonconforming; pressure to conform may cause rebellion; sometimes seen as "different" by peers

12. Humor: views select situations as humorous; enjoys intellectual humor

13. Can become so attracted to self-selected interests that

3. Uses whole body to respond to feelings and experiences
4. Responds to the mood and sense of music
5. Facile in pantomime
6. Enjoys tapping out rhythms
7. Enjoys some form of dance
8. May wish to move about at inopportune times

other fields are overlooked
14. Perfectionism can immobilize efforts

This table is based on a comprehensive review of literature as well as personal educational and psychological practice, 1972–94. CAUTION: No individual should be expected to satisfy *all* of the characteristics within each or within any one domain of giftedness. Rather, the characteristics comprise the broad extent of traits, and the presence of some should be cause for further investigation regarding above average ability in any one of the domains.

Table 2
Program Options

OPTION/ DESCRIPTION	ADVANTAGES	DISADVANTAGES
Accelerated Content due to ability to address more in less time, gifted students are advanced in areas by content	• not elitist because of regular class placement • allows time for gifted student to move ahead at own pace • creates time for self-selected interest-based studies	• training needed for teacher in curriculum streamlining • teacher preparation time likely increased • teacher flexibility required for students to move at own pace
Accelerated Grade due to advanced ability, gifted students skip all or parts of entire grade levels	• allows for continuous progress without boredom • maintains the gifted child within context of "regular" classes, simply at higher than usual grade levels for age	• possible resentment from teachers and other students and their parents • depending on the individual student, problems with social and emotional issues
Advanced Placement preparation for specific content area examination at high school level, enabling gifted students to obtain early collegiate credit (this option available at high school level only)	• allows continuation of studies in content areas matching student ability and interest • work at levels that are more commensurate with ability	• AP curriculum is prescribed so there is little room for additional study • aside from acceleration of content, no individualization based on student need offered
Cluster Groupings gifted students grouped together as a large segment of a regular class by grade level or by subject with a teacher who wants and knows how to meet needs of the gifted	• elitist charges reduced due to regular class placement • continuous contact with other gifted students • continuous contact with other nongifted students	• possible resentment from nongifted students • possible resentment from teachers who are not assigned to gifted students • extensive training of the classroom teacher required

OPTION/ DESCRIPTION	ADVANTAGES	DISADVANTAGES
Community Mentors gifted are placed individually or in small groups for a limited time with an expert in a field of study	• actual exposure to authentic practicing professionals in areas of interest • allows both acceleration and enrichment in interest fields • flexibility of time and how it is spent	• manager required for the coordination of mentor work with rest of curriculum • mentors require training about working with students, methods to use, student needs
Community Resources persons from the community provide enrichment lessons about vocations, hobbies, and areas of interest	• great variety of subjects not usually available in school • whether single sessions or mini-courses, based on actual student interests • tends to build positive public relations	• availability of mentors may be limited • availability of resources may be limited • teaching ability of resources may be questionable • requires manager to set up schedule and follow up
Extra School Time gifted students are placed in additional school classes thanks to either longer days with extra class periods or Saturday or summer classes	• avoids conflict with other school classes • allows for in-depth study in areas of interest • flexible time and space arrangements	• appendage programs are first eliminated when budgets tighten • possible scheduling conflicts for parents and students' out-of-school activities • requires additional funds for teacher time and supplies
Honors Program in-depth courses in every content area with special teachers (secondary schools only)	• allows larger group to be in gifted program due to subject field basis • positive public relations thanks to larger numbers served • instruction appropriate to student needs	• teachers need training in gifted education • usually not much flexibility for students to pursue self-selected, interest-based study

OPTION/ DESCRIPTION	ADVANTAGES	DISADVANTAGES
Itinerant Teacher teacher travels among schools to provide for gifted students	• students have access to teacher with appropriate training • students can develop personal plan of study • allows gifted students to have some contact with each other	• coordination time needed to work with regular classroom teachers and their programs • possible conflicts with regular programs • availability of program may not match times when students most need it
Magnet Programs full-time gifted programming in a school other than the one which neighbors' children typically attend	• full-time gifted program can account for student needs full-time • continual contact with other gifted students • acceleration as well as enrichment are possible	• specific training in gifted education necessary for teachers • allows for charges of elitism with little or no contact with nongifted students • possible resentment from the community
Mini-Courses all students select from a schedule of enrichment classes to be offered on a regular basis for a short period of time	• wide variety of possible subjects allows for interest-based study • due to inclusion of every child, little chance for charges of elitism	• courses reliant on interests and abilities of teachers • scheduling conflicts • transitory nature • no guarantee teachers know anything or care about needs of gifted students
Resource Rooms gifted students visit a specialist on a regular basis for a specified amount of time weekly	• opportunity for in-depth study based on student interests • teacher expressly trained in gifted education • contact with other gifted students on a regular basis	• may conflict with regular class teachers and schedules • requires extra time for coordination with remainder of school •possible resentment from those not included, students and parents alike

OPTION/ DESCRIPTION	ADVANTAGES	DISADVANTAGES
Resource School gifted students attend a school other than the one they usually attend for part of each week	• teacher who specializes in working with gifted students • contact with other gifted students • opportunity for interest-based, in-depth study	• accommodations for gifted students in regular classes are not guaranteed • possible resentment from others • possible conflict with regular school